Ecumenical & Interreligious Perspectives: Globalization in Theological Education

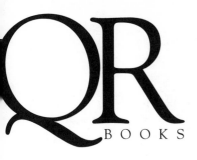
BOOKS

Ecumenical & Interreligious Perspectives: Globalization in Theological Education

RUSSELL E. RICHEY, *Editor*

with an introduction by Robert E. Reber

Nashville

Ecumenical and Interreligious Perspectices:
Globalization in Theological Education

*copyright 1992, The United Methodist Board of Higher Education
and Ministry.*

This book is printed on recycled, acid-free paper.

Library of Congress Catalog Card Number: 91-062662

GENERAL COMMISSION ON CHRISTIAN UNITY AND INTERRELIGIOUS CONCERNS

Seminary Task Force

Dr. Ridgway Shinn, Jr., chair
Retired Professor
Rhode Island College

The Rev. Patricia Farris
United University Church
Los Angeles, California

Dr. Norman E. Dewire, President
Methodist Theological School in Ohio
Delaware, Ohio

Dr. Jean Miller Schmidt
Iliff School of Theology
Denver, Colorada

Bishop William B. Oden
Louisiana Area

Ms. Carol Colley
Ph.D. student
University of California, Berkeley

Dr. Russell E. Richey, Associate Dean for Academic Programs
Duke Divinity School
Durham, North Carolina

The Rev. Thomas Starnes, Director
Council on Ministries
Baltimore Conference
(member, Board of Higher Education and Ministry)

CONTENTS

1 Globalization and the Oikoumene in Theological
   Education
   M. Douglas Meeks 3

2 Family Meal, Holy Communion, and Love Feast:
   Three Ecumenical Metaphors
   Russell E. Richey 17

3 The Local Church and the World:Ecumenical and
   Interreligious Agenda of The United Methodis
   Church
   Roy I. Sano 31

4 United Methodism's Basic Ecumenical Policy
   John Deschner 45

5 Cultivating the Passion for Unity: Four Key Issues in
   the Globalization of Theological Education
   Michael Kinnamon 59

6 The Terminology of Ecumenism and Interreligious
   Dialogue in Theological Education
   Jane I. Smith .... .58

7 Theological Education in Light of the Consultation on
   Church Union
   Diedra H. Kriewald 69

8   The Universal and the Particular in Muslim-
     Christian Dialogue
     Lamin Sanneh 91

9   The Global-Contextual Matrix in the Seminary
     Classroom
     M. Thomas Thangaraj 109

10   Teaching for Ecumenism: A Personal Journey
     Jane Cary Chapman Peck 115

11   Implications of the Yahara Papers for Seminaries
     and for Theological Education
     Ridgway F. Shinn, Jr., and Norman E. Dewire 127

Appendix 1
     Participants in the Consultation on Ecumenical
     Perspectives and Interreligious Dialogue in
     Theological Education
     Yahara Retreat Center, ... 141
     Madison, Wisconsin
     March 22-25, 1990

Appendix 2
     Findings and Observations from the 1987- 88
     Survey of United Methodist Seminaries
     Russell E. Richey and Jean Miller Schmidt 143

PREFACE

A battle rages for the classroom podium and over books in the canon--
the Western classics versus popular, marxist, feminist, non-Western,
African-American writings. That, at least, is the view of sensational
journalism: Higher education rent over multiculturalism and the
literary canon. Actual campus conflict may be less extensive and intense,
may pale beside the picture given in the press. Nevertheless, the
concerns remain important and vexing. What is to be transmitted to the
next generation as our cultural heritage?

Although not receiving quite the sensational press scrutiny, theological education faces its own version of this conflict. It frames such issues
in ways apt for professional/ministerial curricula and concerns.
"Globalization" and "interreligious dialogue" capture some of the current debate, as did "ecumenism" and "missions" still earlier. Discussion
of such matters have dominated the journals devoted to the study of
theological education of late.[1]

Though we should not overlook the similarities to and resonances
with the broader cultural debate, we ought to note that the questions
underlying these issues in the church are neither new nor avoidable.
Indeed, they have been with the church from the start. Paul addressed
them in Romans 9-11. In one way or another, the rest of the New
Testament reflects this struggle, and the church through the ages has
had to wrestle with it as well. How should, how will Christians relate
to the world and to those who call God by various names and in various
fashion?

"Globalization" and "interreligious dialogue" and "ecumenism" are
by no means the only ways to frame such questions. They put in the
imperative what, for some, ought to be debatable, open to question, or
even unthinkable. These terms imply that theological education ought
to take account, perhaps in new and fresh ways, the religious diversity

already present in even the smallest communities in the U.S. and to equip clergy for leadership in what seems an ever smaller world. They issue imperatives for the world and the church's mission to the world. On such matters United Methodists do not think alike, as the intense reaction to recent appointments at one theological school and controversy over missions should indicate. Some experience the imperatives implied in these terms as deeply troubling, even "wrong."

Still, United Methodism cannot readily escape the issues. The Gulf War brought the world of Islam into America's living rooms. Muslims also live just down the street. The relation of church to mosque will command our attention in the years ahead. So also will the relations among synagogue, mosque, and church. American religion will take Hindu and Sikh form, and that of the several religions of Asia. New neighbors pose fresh challenges for United Methodists. Is their conversion the sole route to accord? In the past we certainly thought so. Good converts made good, if distant, neighbors. How will we learn to live with those who have settled in our community, show no desire to be converted, and press their own claims on public school and community protocol?

And there remains unfinished business with old neighbors--with other members of the Methodist/Wesleyan family; with the Protestants now exploring deeper relationships through COCU[2]; with the larger Christian family of local, state, National and World Councils of Churches. Another test of neighborliness is the division within the church, particularly between the evangelical and liberal wings of the denomination. Volatile issues like abortion and sexuality surface quite deep fissures. And beyond the religious family are the neighbors in need, the claims put by poverty, injustice, hunger, war, and by the various "isms": racism, imperialism, sexism. We face diversity. What unity and/or comity we can establish amid diversity? How will we structure our relationship to the world?

Ecumenical issues pertain to policy; they also affect belief and polity. Ecumenism "intrudes" internally in our denominational study commissions, particularly those dealing with sacraments and ministry. Will United Methodism chart its theological and liturgical course cognizant of the commitments it has made on the ecumenical front? Or will it, when faced with hard choices, revert only to Wesleyan formulations? And which shows greater loyalty to the Wesleys--appeal to an ecumenical consensus itself largely normed on the earliest Christian traditions and seeking the unity of Christian hearts, or an appeal to the exact words of the Wesleys? What emphasis should we put on our ecumenical traditions and commitments in fact of severe budgetary and member-

ship numbers within? Does ecumenism divert attention from other
legitimate and seemingly pressing internal matters or might it be the
solution to them?[3] Or to put the question theologically, what constitutes "Tradition" for United Methodism? Is it really the whole Tradition of the church, on which ecumenical formulations now rest? Is it the
Methodist tradition in the last two centuries? Or the earlier traditions
as mediated through Methodism?

The essays in this volume do not settle such issues. Indeed, the
authors differ on priorities and in perspective. Names--globalization,
ecumenism, interreligious dialogue, indigenization, justice, and so
forth--betray those divergences. These essays do, however, open to the
United Methodist Church as a whole debates largely internal in the
seminary world and much of it focused in ATS. They also connect
conversations ongoing in theological education with the discussions in
the church and in the larger society. In so doing, they may well also bring
issues and concerns of church and society to bear upon the seminary.

Written by persons concerned in one way or another with United
Methodism ecumenical relations and theological education, the essays
derive from a consultation held in March 1990 at Yahara, Wisconsin
under the sponsorship of the Division of Ordained Ministry, the General
Commission on Christian Unity and Interreligious Concerns, and the
Association of United Methodist Theological Schools.[4] The consultation
gathered faculty representatives from the United Methodist seminaries,
really for the first time in recent memory, to discuss the issues framed
and named by these essays. From those discussions derived an array of
recommendations to seminaries, AUMTS, DOM and GCCUIC--non-
binding of course--on how to move theological education forward on
these questions. Each of those entities have received the suggestions. A
number of the presentations given at the consultation have appeared in
revised form in *Quarterly Review*. With the financial support of GCCUIC
and DOM and the good offices of Sharon J. Hels, editor of *QR*, these
essays are gathered into this volume as a way of inviting others in the
church to such policy discussions. The selection and editing of the essays
have been undertaken by a committee--Norman E. Dewire, Jeanne
Audrey Powers, Robert E. Reber, Jean Miller Schmidt, Ridgeway F.
Shinn, Jr.--which I have chaired. The committee and editor Sharon Hels
have shaped the volume in ways we hope will serve to further our
thinking on matters ecumenical.

Notes

1. The reference here is to *Theological Education*, the journal of the Association of Theological Schools, and to its national gatherings. Since the mid-1980s, the leadership of this important group has focused attention on globalization and inter-religious dialogue. The level and intensity of this debate can be seen in the essay by Jane I. Smith, "The Terminology of Ecumenism and Interreligious Dialogue in Theological Education."

2. The acronmym is perhaps better known than the organization for which it now stands, The Church of Christ Uniting. Previously termed the Consultation on Church Union, COCU brings together the following churches: the African Methodist Episcopal Church, the African Methodist Episcopal Zion Church, the Christian Church (Disciples of Christ), the Christian Methodist Episcopal Church, the Episcopal Church of the U.S.A., The International Council of Community Churches, the Presbyterian Church (U.S.A.), the United Church of Christ and the United Methodist Church. In an "advisory participant"category are the Evangelical Lutheran Church in American, the Reformed Church in America, and the Roman Catholic Church. The proposals now before the churches are detailed in The COCU Consensus: In Quest of a Church of Christ Uniting and Churches in Covenant Communion, both available from COCU, Princeton, N.J. See also the essay in this volume by Diedra Kriewald, "Theological Education in Light of the Consultation on Church Union."

3. Heightened denominational consciousness, at least partially stimulated by numerical decline, characterizes much of mainstream Protestantism. That does not make our choices any easier, but it should indicate to others that we are aware of being in the same boat with them.

4. Abbreviated hereinafter as DOM, GCCUIC, and AUMTS.

5. The leadership of the sponsoring boards and agencies was also present and played a creative role in the consultation.

INTRODUCTION

Ecumenism is no stranger to theological education. Indeed, it would be the rare seminary today that would operate with an exclusive or denominational orientation. Certainly, United Methodist schools understand themselves as ecumenical. That is hardly surprising, given the common universe of theological scholarship and the diversity of faculties and student bodies. Beyond that, most schools offer courses, lectureships and special events that explicitly touch upon the ecumenical arena--its history, documents, and current discussions.

And yet, there is no agreement at the heart of theological education about the nature of the unity that we seek in the church or in the world, or what a curriculum or pedagogy would look like that is truly ecumenical at its very core. Similarly, the globalization of theological education has been on the agenda of many seminaries and in its name seminaries have revamped curricula, set up exchange programs involving students and faculty from the so-called Third World, engaged in dialogue with people of other faiths, and rewritten catalogues. Despite that, we lack clear agreement on the meaning of globalization and may express a good bit of reservation about using the term at all.

The articles in this volume focus on the larger ecumenical and interreligious agenda of the church in the U.S. and The United Methodist Church in particular; the Consultation on Church Union (COCU); the specific challenge of interreligious dialogue in a global society and in a nation which is marked by increasing plurality; and the globalization of theological education itself within a church that is rooted in the local and open to the global.

What is the future agenda of theological education? In chapter one, "Globalization and the *Oikoumene* in Theological Education," Meeks says that the church requires ecumenicity, interreligious dialogue, and globalization, and that they cannot be separated. All three "mutually coinhere in such a way that to lose one would mean to lose all." He also is firmly convinced that "to hold these crucial realities together will require that our understanding and practice of all three will have to change." We are well into the future agenda but we have a long way to go. Among the questions that Meeks raises are: What would it mean for United Methodist seminaries to begin practicing an intentional and disciplined conciliarity? Where is the teaching office lodged in the denomination and who should carry it out? How do ecumenical, inter-religious, and global concerns become an integrated focus of the seminary as a whole?

Russell Richey's essay entitled "Family Meal, Holy Communion, and Love Feast: Three Ecumenical Metaphors" builds on an interesting nineteenth century Methodist life, feature of the camp meeting, which was sustained by three meals: eucharist or communion, the love feast, and the family meal. He does this "to discover how, as Methodism went about its work, it managed to hold itself together" through the regular practice of having three meals. Richey understands these meals to be expressions, if not the embodiment, of the ideals of ecumenism, evangelism, and justice. He believes that the metaphor of the camp meeting offers a new perspective to Methodists who suffer today from conflicts between liberals and conservatives and battles over differing priorities. In addition, a better understanding of our history and life as Methodists gives us the opportunity to bring something of our own heritage and commitments to the wider ecumenical table.

What do we mean by "ecumenical"? Are we talking about Baptism, Eucharist, and Ministry or Justice, Peace, and the Integrity of Creation or both? What kind of unity do we have in mind? Are we concerned about all humanity or the churches or both? What does it look like at the local or the global level? How do we keep alive the ecumenical memory, the rich history of ecumenical accomplishments in areas of faith and order and life and work? What is the ecumenical commitment of The United Methodist Church? How do we build upon the inter-denominational makeup and global realities already inherent in the experiences of many local church members and realize the gains that have been made for Christian unity? These are the issues that Roy Sano addresses in his essay. His answer is that we begin our ecumenical practice in our own churches, with members who have come from other denominations and may harbor a variety of different points of view.

John Deschner emphasizes repeatedly that "ecumenism is of the essence of United Methodism" and that our denomination faces no more searching questions than those asking about the health of our ecumenical commitments. The stage is set for not allowing any of us off the hook in grappling with enormously challenging issues in every arena of church life. We are reminded by Michael Kinnamon that the ecumenical vision refers to the unity and renewal of the whole Christian Church, its worldwide mission, and the unity of all humankind. All three dimensions are essential to the life of a church which is faithful to the gospel and the ecumenical vision.

Diedra Kriewald writes about the "best kept secret" in the church and theological education: the Consultation on Church Union (COCU). COCU is the covenanting framework in which nine Protestant denominations, including The United Methodist Church, have reached a historic theological agreement on the apostolic faith; covenantal communion in faith, sacraments, ministry, and mission; and a revolutionary concept of a new ecclesial reality called the Church of Christ Uniting. United Methodism must seriously consider the COCU Consensus if it is to deal responsibly with questions concerning denominational identity.

One of the greatest challenges that we face is how to think theologically about the faith of our neighbors, whether they be Jewish, Buddhist, Hindu, or Muslim, and about our own faith in the context of our neighbors' faith. The plurality of religious faiths is not only a given in our world but a rapidly growing phenomenon within the U.S. In this context what does dialogue involve? How should we witness to our faith in Christ? What should be the mission of the church at home and around the world? How does the church, and theological education in particular, respond to the plurality, the diversity, and interdependence of the human community and the planet on which we must learn to live together?

In chapter 8, "The Universal and the Particular in Muslim-Christian Dialogue," Lamin Sanneh challenges us to pay attention to what Third World Christians have learned from their experience of living and ministering in a profoundly pluralist religious and cultural world. "Whereas Western Christians often make the assumption that religious pluralism occurred after the formulations of Christianity had been put in place, Third World Christians know their Christianity is a part of and a consequence of pluralism." Sanneh points to Kenneth Cragg as one who, in the area of Muslim-Christian dialogue, has understood that Christians must be clear about their own religious commitments in order to seek reconciliation with those of another faith.

It is certainly clear in the chapters by Smith and Thangaraj how problematic the term "globalization" is. Some see it as a way to do contextual theology. Others think its aim is to understand the mission of the church as both local and global. Then there are those who talk about globalization as a process that leads to concrete forms and expressions of solidarity in religious, geopolitical, and economic terms. Some make the judgment that it is a form of Western imperialism. Whatever position one takes, we must be willing to examine the theological and pedagogical implications of globalization. There is little doubt that we are in for some massive upheavals in theological education that include both seminary and local church.

Norman Dewire and Ridgeway Shinn provide an excellent analysis of major themes and issues emerging from the six working groups at the Yahara Consultation. They identify directions for further theological, curricular, and pedagogical study, reflection, and action.

The consultation on Ecumenism, Interreligious Dialogue, and Theological Education could not have been more timely. The survey (see Appendix 2) by Richey and Schmidt of curricular offerings and their analysis of catalogues of United Methodist seminaries indicate considerable commitment to ecumenism, globalization, and interreligious dialogue, and a need to address a number of questions at the very heart of theological education and the life of the church.

Hopefully, this sampling of ideas, concerns, and questions whets the reader's appetite for the articles that follow. It also is intended to give some idea of how diverse and rich the Consultation on Ecumenism, Interreligious Dialogue and Theological Education was. The schedule was extremely full, including major addresses, opportunities for discussion with speakers and participants in small groups, worship, and meal times for getting better acquainted. Six working groups met throughout the consultation: Ecclesial Agreements (BEM, COCU, Bilateral Dialogues with Roman Catholics and Lutherans): Reception in Church and Seminary; Denominational Formation and Ecumenical Formation; Developing the Next Generation of Ecumenical Leadership: How Should It Be Undertaken? What Role Should the Seminary Play?; Ministerial Formation in an Increasingly Interreligious Context; The Terminology of Unity: Meanings, Relationships, Conflicts and Priorities; and The Theological Impact and Adequacy of Globalization. The reports from these groups provide many ideas and suggestions to keep all concerned about theological education in its broadest terms busy well into the year 2000.

From the very beginning, the consultation was conceived as a joint venture by the Division of Ordained Ministry of the Board of Higher Education and Ministry and the General Commission on Christian Unity and Interreligious Concerns in cooperation with the Association of United Methodist Schools. Such joint sponsorship and planning is crucial among agencies in The United Methodist Church.

All thirteen seminaries had faculty representatives at the consultation. Six deans and three presidents were among their ranks. Eleven elected directors and staff from the two sponsoring agencies, including three bishops, participated fully in the deliberations. While focused only on United Methodist Seminaries, we were delighted to discover how ecumenically diverse the faculties have become. Although United Methodists were in abundance, other communions represented were African Methodist Episcopal, Disciples of Christ, Episcopal, Presbyterian, United Church of Canada, United Church of Christ, Greek Orthodox, and the Church of South India. The leadership, too, included persons from Andover-Newton Theological School, Auburn Theological Seminary, Eden Theological Seminary, Lexington Theological Seminary, and Yale Divinity School.

In many respects what is presented in the articles to come is what we need to think and pray about. Readers will not find typical conference reports but rather scholars who are deeply committed church members wrestling with ideas and issues that are at the very heart of church life and theological education today. They are ecumenists who believe that God surely wills the unity of the Church and the unity of all humankind. They differ on approaches and theological perspectives. No facile answers or simple solutions are offered--only an invitation to a journey that requires the best of each of us as we learn together what ecumenism, interreligious dialogue, and globalization are all about, and what God is calling us to be as faithful Christians in our time.

Ecumenical & Interreligious Perspectives: Globalization in Theological Education

GLOBALIZATION AND THE OIKOUMENE IN THEOLOGICAL EDUCATION

M. DOUGLAS MEEKS

There hang in my office two pictures I found in East Berlin in the late sixties, when I was doing research on European political theology. They have helped me come to grips with the difficulties of relating Christian faith and the world's claims to truth and power. Both pictures depict a fool. In the first the fool is walking beside the king. We see them from behind, their heads bowed in deep conversation, their hands folded behind them, a scepter in the hands of the king, a fool's cap in his companion's. The fool, one could assume, is speaking the truth to power. But they are walking in a secluded garden where no one else can hear their conversation. The other picture is of the fool *zwischen den Stuhlen*, "between the chairs," a German colloquialism for the state of being perplexed and ambivalent. The dazed smile on the face of the fool befits the confusion of falling between conflicting claims.

These two states of the fool may have some application to theological education and the church of our time. This is certainly not the first time in history that a transition period has produced uncertainty about how to speak the claims of Jesus Christ truthfully in a world content with its own claims and how to live with the ambivalence created in the household of the seminary and church by conflicting claims of the household's own members. Even if, as it is, the uncertainty is accompanied by excitement and the anticipation of new shapes of theological education, it is nevertheless proper to remember that many who have gone before us in such times thought discipleship something like being a "fool for Christ."

Seminary faculties learned in the eighties that the customary way of putting together the theological curriculum has been debilitating for the ministry and mission of the church.[1] The integrity of theological education, it was argued, should not be based on the methodologies of the academic fields or the professionalization of clergy. The present debate suggests that the unity and integrity of theological education should rather lie somewhere in the *oikoumene*, globalization, and interreligious dialogue. But we have fallen "between the chairs." We have discovered that there is a conflict of interpretations among us. We have sensed that the ecumenical movement, globalization, and interreligious dialogue, as they are being commonly understood, *do* compete with each other in theological education and in the church. We understand ecumenicity, globalization, interreligious dialogue differently depending on our position on the foundational questions of particularity and universality, relativity and constancy, plurality and unity, inclusivity and exclusivity, evangelism and dialogue, identity and justice.

Those who love the ecumenical movement worry that the movement seems to be floundering and wonder why we are not better able to engender its future. What we have loved is either forgotten or scorned as passe. Our perplexity is deepened by the widely shared conviction that The United Methodist Church is essentially and necessarily ecumenical.[2] It belongs constitutionally to the church uniting movement. The United Methodist Church's peculiar heritage is constitutive of the church universal. What is distinctive to us are trusts to be shared with the whole church. If this is the case, as I believe it is, the fate of the ecumenical movement is of more than passing concern for United Methodists.

But we are "between the chairs." On one side is the generation of great visionaries of the one visibly united church of Jesus Christ. Their vivid depictions of the yet open promises of the ecumenical movement still grip and stir us. Theological educators often feel at fault for the failure to inform our students about the ecumenical mandate of the church and to help them to become practical ecumenists. We yearn for a new commitment. But on the other side are our students and children and people all over the world struggling for freedom from political, economic, and cultural oppression, a generation for whom these ecumenical visions and language have become suspect.

What has become problematic for so many people about ecumenical language? The language of ecumenicity stresses *unity*. Unity is a political term, which is to say it is a term of power. The suspicions about the ecumenical movement center around the false unification of the church culturally, racially, ethnically, or nationally. Aristotle articulated in his *Nicomachean Ethics* the oldest and most successful theory of sociality: "Birds of the feather flock together." Many Christians throughout the world do not want unity in terms defined from the perspectives of northern, white, male, industrial dominance. Many are committed to work against such unity. No unity without justice. The World Council of Churches meeting in Canberra, Australia, was perhaps a watershed revealing that we cannot go further without radical changes in the ecumenical movement. And yet we cannot go further in globalization without what has been gained in the ecumenical movement. Indeed, the irony is that the ecumenical movement has itself wakened in us the consciousness of cultural and religious diversity that is now claimed by some to be underrepresented in the ecumenical movement.

Within North American theological education "globalization" is the current rallying cry.[3] But how are we to understand globalization? Is "globalization" meant to supercede the ecumenical movement? Is "globalization" a new word for ecumenicity and mission? Does globalization mean that social and economic justice in the global community is the irreducible core of theological education? Is "interreligious and intercultural dialogue" the central meaning of "globalization" so that it should supercede both ecumenicity and globalization as the key to theological education?[4]

I do not believe that globalization should jettison the ecumenical movement. In fact we are far enough along in the debate to say that globalization and interreligious dialogue are not panaceas for theological education; they do not in themselves solve the major questions facing us. The future of the church requires all of these realities (ecumenicity, globalization, interfaith dialogue). Indeed, it seems to me that they mutually coinhere in such a way that to lose one would mean to lose all. But to hold these crucial realities together will require that our understanding and practice of all three will have to change.

Oikos as Key for Relating *Oikoumene*, Globalization, and Interreligious Dialogue

I submit that *oikoumene* should remain the key term, even as we appropriate the new perceptions and experiences generated by globalization and interfaith dialogue. But the meaning of *oikoumene* has to be expanded. If the ecumenical movement is going to have a future, it will look different from what we have known and will have to be related inherently to globalization and the community of the world religions as well as more intentionally to the life of the congregation.

The word *oikoumene*, connected with *oikos* (household, home), belongs to our oldest memories and richest language systems.[5] *Oikos* provides the root meaning not only for *oikoumene* but also for economy and ecology. It is in these three spheres that the survival of the globe will be determined. All of these terms are about home. Home is where people know your name, where they can tell your story and therefore

5

join with you in anticipating your future. All things in nature also need a name and a history if they are to survive. Having a home means being confronted, forgiven, loved, and hoped for. It means having a place at the table and a claim on sharing what is on the table. Fundamentally, home means access to what it takes to live and live abundantly. To be homeless is to be subjected to death.

The life and death questions of *oikos* have been largely repressed under our modern fascination with progress.[6] So caught up are we in our implicit faith in mechanistic theories of economy that the questions of *oikos*, in their ancient sense, no longer seem sophisticated enough. And yet they are starkly real and irreducible. The question of economy is, will everyone in the household have access to what it takes to live and live abundantly? The question of ecology is, will nature have a home, its own living space? The question of the *oikoumene* is, will the peoples of the earth be able to inhabit the earth in peace? Taken together they constitute *oikoumene* as the most comprehensive horizon for the church's service of God's redemption of the world. These are questions of creative justice, that is, God's power of life against death.

Oikoumene, then, comprises not just the unity of the church but God's oikic work to make the world into a home. As all narrations of its history make clear, the modern ecumenical movement came out of the practice of mission. The theme is still the same: How can the church be prepared to serve God's oikic work?

Why, then, has globalization come on the scene? Globalization and interreligious dialogue stress the difficulty of creating home across cultural, social, political, and religious differences. They question the particularistic and sometimes dominating thrust of Christian mission. In some forms they eschew mission altogether and downplay the tradition in order to find an unmediated universal truth, a world theology. They want to proceed directly to a universal community without taking the difficult path of conversion. What is missing in many of these current understandings of globalization and interreligious dialogue is our own conversion. For fear of a narrow absolutist approach in ecumenical circles, there is a tendency to opt for yet another absolutist approach.[7] The approach we should follow, it seems to me, is to take seriously the new ground plowed by globalization and interreligious dialogue in order to bring these experiences into a transformed practice of the *oikoumene*.

The Necessity of Globalization

Globalization is a term that has risen from the economic universe of discourse, which is ruled by multinational corporations in the United

States, the European Common Market, and Japan. It is based on the recognition that local and national economies are increasingly tenuous, that is, that governments are less and less capable of holding economic actors accountable to the humanity and dignity of the people in their sphere of influence.

Despite the cry for democracy now heard round the world, the great global enterprises that make the key decisions--about what people eat and drink, what they read and hear, what sort or air they breathe and water they drink, and, ultimately, which societies will flourish and which city blocks will decay--are becoming less and less accountable to the people whose lives they change. Global corporations, whatever flag they fly, have outgrown national laws and national cultures, and the whole world has not begun to address the problem.[8]

From this perspective, globalization, then, means that there is one global economy and that those who can comprehend or control the household rules of the global economy, its language and logic, its resource allocation, and its markets will survive and be secure. Those who do not globalize will increasingly become victims of an irreversible historical process. And thus we have the recent self-congratulatory claim of a major multinational corporation, "We globalized forty years ago!"

But a full two-thirds of people in the global household, the majority of people in Asia, Africa, and Latin America and an increasing proportion of marginalized persons in the first world, are being left out of the global household and hence are increasingly threatened with hopeless conditions of death. Those who are systemically excluded from the North American public household are also subject to death.[9] Shall we consider it an irony that within North American theological education "globalization" has become the current rallying cry?

The *absolutist approach* in globalization and interreligious relationships can make it impossible for us to see what, in my opinion, is the greatest threat to the church's freedom for the gospel and its power for mission to the *oikoumene* (which includes freedom for interreligious community in our time), namely, the universal and totalitarian reality of the *market society*.[10] To be sure, the market is in itself a good human instrument. But when market logic spreads into all dimensions of the world's societies, freedom is denied. If we really want to speak of globalization in relation to God's oikic mission, then we must face the fact that market logic determines all spheres of social goods, and thereby excludes many people from what it takes to live and live abundantly. When unity is defined by the market logic, the interpretation of scripture and formulation of doctrine become ideological, that is, a means of promoting one's own interests at the expense of another. These inter-pretations can cloak or condone an unconscious desire to maintain superiority or to dominate, control, or devalue other traditions. Ideologized doctrines and practices used to justify the subordination and exploitation of other cultures and religions have to be detected and revised before God's word can be heard. Such an ecclesial task is nothing less than global in scope.

Globalization therefore entails a disciplined awareness of the new world context in which theology and church must live. It also encom-passes the search for new modalities of theology, church life, and mission in the world. Globalization as such does not provide new criteria for theology. It does not present an occasion in which the Christian tradition should or can be suddenly discarded. Globalization, in con-tradistinction from the spreading of the universal logics of the market, of progress, of deterrence, and of the exploitation of nature, should mean living *coram Deo* in the modality of the gospel at this time in history in this place in the world household.

The Gospel as the Focus and Criterion of Globalization

The ecclesiological work of globalization and mission to the *oikoumene* is grounded in the power of God's word, which has the shape of the gospel. I believe that theological education as *oikoumene* renewed through globalization and interreligious dialogue can find its integrity and empowerment only in the gospel. If globalization requires radically new analyses of the world context of theological education, it also requires a steady focus on the gospel, without which it has no theological content and direction and can easily serve, if unsuspectingly, the globalization of the market society. Simply to say the word *gospel* does not end the debate about globalization, but it clarifies, I believe, what the argument is about.

Gospel (*euaggelion*) has at least two basic meanings or dimensions: the good news proclaimed by Jesus and the good news which is Jesus.

(1) The good news proclaimed by Jesus he received from the tradi-tions of our older Scriptures: God's righteousness reigns. Jesus added the timing: *Today* God's righteousness is at hand, in your midst. "Righteousness," God's power for life against death, is the means by which God creates home for God's creation.

The shape of the gospel, which Jesus as a member of the household of Israel received and proclaimed, is promise and command. The promise is that the conditions for life against death are being created by the righteousness and power of God in the midst of history. If the promise of the gospel is the presence of God's righteousness/justice (Immanuel), then the command of the gospel is mission to the *oikoumene* which God will redeem. The promise of God's righteousness and God's sending (mission) to serve the life of the *oikoumene* are constitutive of a household which trusts and lives from the good news.

Concretely this means that globalized theological education should find its practical integrating focus in the congregation's mission to the *oikoumene*.[11]

(2) The second sense of good news is Jesus himself as grounded in the resurrection of the crucified one. The good news is that the character of God has the shape of Jesus and his future. This is good news in at least three senses:

(a) The power by which righteousness can be done is radically different from all other kinds of power, all of which tend to destroy themselves and various aspects of God's creation. This power is called love and its logic is grace. The power and logic for life are enfleshed in the past, present, and future of Jesus (which embrace Israel, God's creation, and God's universal redemption).

Concretely this means that theological education must engage in the conflict created by the public announcement of the gospel. If the power and logic to which the gospel witnesses are true, then the seminary is responsible for helping the church engage in the strife of conflicting powers and logics in the world. Globalization is a way of saying that these conflicts over the truth of powers and logics are at once local and worldwide.

(b) The power by which justice can be done comes first to the those threatened with evil and death (the *am ha-aretz, ptochoi, ochlos*) for no other reason except the character of God who gives it. This character is grace: good news to the poor, justice to the oppressed, name to the nameless, forgiveness to the sinner, sight to the blind, daily bread to the hungry, reconciliation to the enemy. The gospel always appears in relation to those who are excluded from what it takes to live and live abundantly. That is, its oikic shape makes possible the *oikos* of Jesus Christ.

Concretely this means that globalized theological education shaped by the gospel cannot happen apart from people of color, the poor, women, the handicapped, the nameless, prisoners, the unorganized, the uninformed. The poetics, aesthetics, and rhetoric of globalized theological education will arise from the discourses of these people as they struggle for inclusion in the household and radical transformation of the relations and structures of the household.[12]

9

(c) The third sense in which Jesus is the good news is that God is constituted by the community of relationships that appears in the history of Jesus (past, present, and future). Jesus' relationships to Abba and to the Holy Spirit are not only the means of knowing God; they comprise God. There is no God behind or under this community of righteousness. God as a community of righteousness is good news, for this reality is the undermining of all theories and practices of domination, especially the modern ideologies of individualism and privatism.[13] Concretely this means that globalized theological education is a constant practical and theoretical struggle before God for a life that conforms to the character of God's life. Among other things this entails the seminary's attempt to resource the church, and itself as a part of the church, to become a community of diversity and unity that conforms, under the conditions of history, to the Triune Community's own life. A globalized seminary will work for the formation of a household whose household rules are shaped by the gospel, a household which practices hospitality to the homeless in a global setting.

In my judgment, the transformation of the ecumenical movement through globalization is most at risk in the attempt to revive Enlightenment standards of relativism, pluralism, and secularism as the criteria for interreligious and intercultural dialogue.

The Search for Interreligious Community

The absolutism of the Christian church came to an end through the wars of religion and was replaced by the relativism of the Enlightenment and by humanism. But the Enlightenment tradition has its own weaknesses. And those problems have to do with the resulting history of the great Enlightenment clarion calls of tolerance, plurality, relativity, and secularity. Tolerance has become indifference, plurality empty pluralism, relativity relativism, and secularity secularism. Relativism is always married to a hidden absolutism. In most instances a religious relativism seems simply a cloak for a new absolutism. Absolutism and relativism are twins because both view everything from a higher, nohistorical watchtower, a privileged position. In short, the Enlightenment has its own problems of absolutism and triumphalism that lead to a new absolutism.[14]

An affirmation of religious pluralism can all too easily lead us to tolerate what is intolerable. As Paul Knitter has put it:

The First World theologians are well aware that their dialogues have often taken place on mountain tops overlooking barrios and death squads. Theologians engaged in dialogue are realizing that religion that does not address, as a primary concern, the poverty and oppression and ecological degradation that infest our world is not authentic religion. Dialogues between inauthentic religions easily become a purely mystical pursuit or an interesting pastime affordable only by First World mystics or scholars. Something essential is missing in such otherworldly or *ultra academic dialogue.*[15]

Interreligious conversation can easily degenerate into relativistic pap in which "many" means "any" and no one can make any valuative judgments.

How are we to deal with relativism? One way is to move to a universal position, one that penetrates beneath all the accidental and historical differences among human beings and their religions to some supposed essential oneness which we share. Then on the basis of this unity underlying everything human, we can understand and negotiate the differences with which the several great religious traditions confront us.

But there is really no such universally human position available to us; every religious or secular understanding and way of life we might uncover is a *particular* one. Does there have to be a positing of some *common ground* shared by all religions? A common essence within all traditions or a universal faith? Or a common yet indefinable mystical center? We should be warned against positing a common anything within religions as a basis for dialogue.[16] We should resist the search for a foundation or common ground above or outside the plurality of views. There may be no way outside a tradition to assess the meaning and truth of claims made within it.

If we really want to take plurality seriously, then we should cease our search for a universal theory or a common source of religion--or even for one God within all religions.[17] "The problem is the quest for what is common. Truly to accept pluralism is to abandon the quest. If liberal theists really wish to be open, they should simply be open. The openness is inhibited by the need to state in advance what we have in common."[18] There is no one ultimate within or behind all the world religions. In our desire to establish or distill a common essence or center, we all too often miss what is genuinely different, and therefore what is genuinely challenging or frightening in the other. By proposing a universal deity instead of beginning with the particularity of Jesus Christ and Israel as our starting point for dialogue, we are implicitly, unconsciously, but still imperialistically imposing our notions of deity or the ultimate on other believers who, like many Buddhists, may not even wish to speak of God or who experience the ultimate as Sunyata, which has nothing or little to do with what Christians experience and call God.

The commitment to enter into dialogue with the other religions must be found within the particularity of each religion. Only in this way can the domination of one religion over others or the domination of a new umbrella religion be prevented. But this requires that we be true and loyal to the particularity of the other as well as our own particularity. Genuine community requires real diversity. Dialogue cannot be determined by arbitrary and predetermined attitudes. This means that dialogue should begin with a hermeneutic of suspicion, not about the dialogue partner but about one's own religious presuppositions. The search for a genuine freedom for dialogue begins with my struggle for freedom from my own personal, class, national, racial, and gender interests. Are my assumptions simply girding up my ideology by which I express and protect my own interests? The leading question is the ancient question, *Cui bono*? For whose good does the interreligious dialogue exist? Whose interests is it serving? We do not enter into community without a sense of our own incompleteness, without the realization that we are coming to receive something as well as give something.

But if there is no common essence or ground or ultimate that can be predefined, what is common that brings us together? We also should not fall into skepticism and relativism that lock each religion into its own language game. What is the bridge, the table, the common ground, the forum? On what basis can dialogue take place so that the freedom proper to every religion can be safeguarded?

I think the answer is human suffering. Human suffering is a central problem in all world religions. Each confronts the sufferings of humanity and the need to put an end to godless and inhuman relations of the world. The primary components of the religions' community of suffering are compassion, justice, and peace. Compassion or suffering love is the divinely given power to turn to the world. The first sense of suffering is being acted upon, being the object of pain. The second sense of suffering is the power of life, the strength of living. It is the power to go outside of oneself and be with the other. But human suffering remains an open question. No religion has been able to give a definitive answer. Is the problem of suffering "solved when the Buddhist tries to extinguish the 'desire' of life as the ground of suffering? Is it solved if the animist sees it as a disturbance in the cosmic balance and tries to put the disturbance right through sacrifice? Is it solved when the Moslem accepts his or her destiny in total self-surrender to God? Is it solved if the Christian accepts suffering in the love of God and transforms it by virtue of his [or her] hope?"[19] No one of these answers is completely satisfactory.

Compassion turns us to the world where the other is suffering. And there all religions find in common tasks of justice. We go out to encounter other religions, not primarily to enjoy diversity but first of all to work for justice. Justice takes precedence over relativism and pluralism. Life with the poor and the marginalized constitutes the necessary and primary purpose of dialogue. Religions must speak and act together because only when they do so can they make their crucially important contribution to removing the oppression that contaminates the earth.[20]

Returning to the Oikoumenic Task

Globalization and interreligious dialogue will, I believe, take theological education back to renewed work for the oikoumenic church. The ecumenical movement has been right in its argument that community must precede justice, that without community there can be no mutually shared conception of justice or means of establishing justice.[21] Oneness is a gift to be received; being comes before action. But there can be no genuine unity in Christ without transformation. And therefore we must decry the false ecumenicity which replaces unity through *transformation* of the churches with unity as interchurch cooperation.[22] Ecumenical work that elevates Enlightenment tolerance instead of mutual transformation and growth in Christ toward deeper *koinonia* fails the unity to which the church is called.

The ecumenical movement has also reminded us that the root of oppression is not just unjust structures but sin, which can be healed only in the koinonia created by God's grace. Therefore, that oneness of community is the means to mission.[23] Nothing changes for the good in history without living relationship in dialogue, continuing conversation, face-to-face reciprocity, community of shared suffering working for justice. Life in fellowship, life in dialogue changes the atmosphere. Each religion should show its truth and vocation in relationship, in dialogue. Dialogue is not merely a way of discussing suffering; it is also a way of practicing our attitudes to suffering with one another.

But this means, above all, our own transformation: spiritually, socially, and economically. Mutual participation and cross-fertilization become possible only when we understand that such a community will change us. All genuine encounter is transformation. That doesn't mean that we will substitute our most basic beliefs or our traditions, but the way we appropriate our beliefs and traditions will be changed in community. Such a relationship is what our culture and (as far as I know) every culture calls friendship. Interreligious dialogue is a sign of hope

13

for the future of the world if it is carried on in the interests of life and liberation.

This freedom for community among the religions brings about a feast of unending joy. Reconciled human beings of the many religions can find inestimable joy in their reconciliation and in their common compassion for the suffering of the world, for this new community will already be a sign of religious freedom and joy in anticipation of what all the religions know will come one day: a human community of peace with God, with each other, and with nature. To know this freedom already, under the conditions of evil in the world, is a joy for which we should be ready to sacrifice and work with our whole beings.

Despite our having fallen between the chairs, there is abroad in theological education today an extraordinary good will and an energizing hope that we can become generative, that we can occasion the generation of the generations in the *oikoumene*, globalization, and interreligious dialogue. It is time that United Methodist seminaries begin practicing an intentional and disciplined *conciliarity* for the sake of God's *oikoumene*. Whether this work looks like that of a fool, of course, depends not only on one's vantage point in the *oikoumene* but more importantly on the timing of God's gracious righteousness.

Notes

[Editor's note: Authors' references to essays found in this volume but originally published in *Quarterly Review* have been allowed to stand. Their book chapter equivalents are cited in every full reference to the essay.]

1. See especially Edward Farley, *Theologia: The Fragmentation and Unity of Theological Education* (Philadelphia: Fortress, 1983); idem, *The Fragility of Knowledge: Theological Education in the Church and the University* (Philadelphia: Fortress Press, 1988); Joseph C. Hough, Jr., and John B. Cobb, Jr., *Christian Identity and Theological Education* (Chico, Cal.: Scholars Press, 1985); Charles M. Wood, *Vision and Discernment: An Orientation in Theological Study* (Atlanta: Scholars Press, 1985); Rebecca S. Chopp, "Emerging Issues and Theological Education," *Theological Education* 26/2 (Spring 1990), 106-24.

2. The case has been made definitively, among others, by two of our chief ecumenical theologians, Albert Outler and John Deschner. If these claims are true, one avenue for our entering the Church of Christ Uniting (an inclusive, visible, eucharistic community through mutual recognition of ministries and members) lies at hand, for example, in COCU, were we able to abandon our stubborn Methodist claims to self-sufficiency. One sense of malaise arises from the fact that, having given such decisive leadership to the COCU process, The United Methodist Church seems now to be expressing reluctance.

3. In addition to the literature given in Russell E. Richey, "Globalization in Theological Education," *Quarterly Review* 11/1 (Spring 1991), 58-68 - Appendix 2, see "Fundamental Issues in Globalization," *Theological Education* 26/Supplement 1 (Spring 1990) and "Patterns of Globalization: Six Studies," *Theological Education* 27/2 (Spring 1991).

4. See S. Mark Heim, "Mapping Globalization for Theological Education," *Theological Education* 26/Supplement 1 (Spring 1990), 7-34. Heim argues that globalization will be understood according to the perspective one occupies regarding evangelization, mission/*oikoumene*, social justice, and dialogue with the other religions and that one's perspective will be further refined by one's predilection to a specific type(s) of social analysis.

5. M. Douglas Meeks, *God the Economist: The Doctrine of God and Political Economy* (Minneapolis: Fortress Press, 1989), 2-4, 33-37.

6. Christopher Lasch, *The True and Only Heaven: Progress and Its Critics* (New York: W.W. Norton, 1991).

7. Mark Kline Taylor and Gary J. Bekker offer a sobering caveat to simplified views of "globalization," in "Engaging the Other in a Global Village," *Theological Education* 26/Supplement 1 (Spring 1990), 52-83.

8. Richard Barnet, "Defining the Moment," *The New Yorker* (July 16, 1990), 46-60.

9. See Robert B. Reich, *The Work of Nations: Preparing Ourselves for 21st Century Capitalism* (New York: Alfred A. Knopf, 1991).

10. Here I draw on Karl Polanyi's careful distinctions between a market economy and a market society. See his *The Great Transformation* (Boston: Beacon Press, 1957) and *The Livelihood of Man* (New York: Academic Press, 1977).

11. The recent proposals for the congregation as the integrating focus of theological education go in the right direction, but in general they do not stress enough the mission of the congregation in the global context of injustice. See James F. Hopewell, *Congregation: Stories and Structures*, ed. Barbara G. Wheeler (Philadelphia: Fortress Press, 1987); Joseph C. Hough and Barbara G. Wheeler, Jr., *Beyond Clericalism: The Congregation as a Focus for Theological Education* (Atlanta: Scholars Press, 1988); Letty M. Russell raises particularly pertinent questions in "Which Congregation? A Mission Focus for Theological Education," in *Beyond Clericalism*, pp. 31-35. See also James A. Scherer, *Gospel, Church, and Kingdom: Comparative Studies in World Mission Theology* (Minneapolis: Augsburg, 1987).

12. Cf. Rebecca S. Chopp, *The Power to Speak: Feminism, Language, God* (New York: Crossroad, 1989).

13. This means that exigency for the unity of the church and the justice of the *oikoumene* is found in the fundamental logic of the Christian faith, the life of the Triune Community. For an extended argument see M. Douglas Meeks, *God the Economist*.

14. Cf. the arguments of Lamin Sanneh in "Religious Particularity in Muslim-Christian Dialogue," *Quarterly Review* 11/2 (Summer 1991), 40-60 chapter 8, ("The Universal and the Particular in Muslim-Christian Dialogue.")

15. Paul F. Knitter, "Toward a Liberation Theology of Religion," in *The Myth of Christian Uniqueness: Toward a Pluralistic Theology of Religions* (Maryknoll, N.Y.: Orbis Books, 1987), 180.

16. "By 'objectivism' I mean the basic conviction that there is or must be some permanent ahistorical matrix or framework to which we can ultimately appeal in determining the nature or rationality, knowledge, truth, reality, goodness, or rightness [and religious experience]....Objectivism is closely related to foundationalism and the search for an Archimedean point. The objectivist maintains that unless we can ground philosophy, knowledge, or language in a rigorous manner, we cannot avoid radical skepticism." Jeremy Bernstein, *Beyond Objectivism and Relativism: Science, Hermeneutics, and Praxis* (Philadelphia: University of Pennsylvania Press, 1983). See also Richard Rorty, *Philosophy and the Mirror of Nature* (Princeton: Princeton University Press, 1979).

17. According to Raimundo Pannikar, "Pluralism does not allow for a universal system. A pluralist system would be a contradiction in terms. The incommensurability of ultimate systems is unbridgeable."

18. John B. Cobb, *Beyond Dialogue: Toward a Mutual Transformation of Christianity and Buddhism* (Philadelphia: Fortress Press, 1982), 86-90; 110-14; cf. idem, "Buddhist Emptiness and the Christian God." *Journal of the American Academy of Religion* 45 (1979), 11-25.

19. Jurgen Moltmann, *The Church in the Power of the Spirit*, trans. Margaret Kohl (San Francisco: Harper & Row, 1977), 161.

20. "Economic, political, and especially nuclear liberation is too big a job for any one nation, or culture, or religion....A worldwide liberation movement needs a worldwide interreligious dialogue." Paul F. Knitter, "Toward a Liberation Theology of Religions," in *The Myth of Christian Uniqueness: Toward a Pluralistic Theology of Religions*, ed. John Hick and Paul F. Knitter (Maryknoll, N.Y.: Orbis Books, 1987).

21. See M. Douglas Meeks, "Love and the Hope for a Just Society" in *Love: The Foundation of Hope*, ed. Frederic Burham, Charles McCoy, and M. Douglas Meeks (San Francisco: Harper & Row, 1988), 41-59. This argument is also made convincingly by Michael Walzer, *Spheres of Justice* (New York: Basic Books, 1985).

22. See Michael Kinnamon, "Globalization in Theological Education: Naming the Issues in Ecumenical Perspectives and Interreligious Dialogue," *Quarterly Review* 11/1 (Spring 1991): 73.

23. John Deschner, "United Methodism's Basic Ecumenical Policy," *Quarterly Review* 11/3 (Fall 1991): 44 Chapter 4, ("United Methodism's Basic Ecumenical Policy.")

FAMILY MEAL, HOLY COMMUNION, AND LOVE FEAST:

Three Ecumenical Metaphors

RUSSELL E. RICHEY

In a Christmas-season Sunday school class, a couple confesses how difficult the season has become now that their daughter has married a Muslim. Customs, seasonal observances, and family beliefs must be individually negotiated. They ask for the prayers and support of the class. The larger human family impinges on, indeed divides, their immediate family. Members of a council on ministries meet to struggle over the priority to be given to witness, evangelism, and church growth against new preschool ventures. Despite or without the oversight of the work area of education, Sunday school teachers proceed to order a wide variety of church school materials, including some from the Bristol Bible Curriculum. The work area chairperson of church and society raises a serious question at a council on ministries meeting. Should all of the church's efforts in urban ministries be mediated through an inter-denominational agency (which the church had itself brought into being)? Would it not be preferable for the church to undertake some missional efforts on its own? The agonies of ecumenism take local expression.

United Methodism is divided by the very ideals which aspire to unite it. Justice, evangelism, and ecumenism--to name but the obvious--would each pull Methodism together around itself. But the ideal and the endeavor to press for it produce not unity but division. The competition on behalf of the three creates cacophony. How might the discord be lessened?[1]

To think about these ideals and their relation, we propose a metaphor--three meals eaten at early American camp meetings: the family meal, the love feast, and the eucharist. Each had, we will propose, its own table, its own community, its own covenant, its own function, and if license be permitted, its own "grace." Methodists could not do without any. The camp meeting offered sustenance for each and all.

17

Before exploring the three meals and the sustenance we might today draw from them or their counterparts, we need to essay the problem more fully.

The Search for Unity

United Methodism does find itself divided by the very ideals which aspire to unite it. Justice, evangelism and ecumenism offer themselves as the sole priority in terms of which Methodism should conceive its mission. Each has its champions. And at every level of church life, the champions contest for position and priority on the denominational agenda. The contest is inescapable; it is built into the organizational fabric. The church itself is structured top to bottom with boards, agencies, committees, and caucuses committed to these ideals. Church and Society, Religion and Race, COSROW, and, to some extent, Global Ministries pursue the various justice issues. Discipleship, Global Ministries, and Good News raise the banner of missions, witness and evangelism. Christian Unity and Interreligious Concerns labors for its ideals with some encouragement from the Council of Bishops. Each agency and its counterparts on every level can be counted upon to press its agenda. But within each, the other ideals emerge, spontaneously, reflexively, to vie for preeminence. The struggle for missional priorities in church, as in the nation, has long since gone beyond the spirited give-and-take that warranted building these distinct ideals into the Methodist machinery.

In its most ferocious expression--the caucuses--the struggle leads to anathemas. So Good News pledged itself in 1990 to the "DuPage Declaration," which delineated the lines of division and ideological rectitude sharply through affirmations and denials. Two of the latter bear citation:

We deny that other religions are pathways to salvation, or that one can be in a right relationship with God apart from repentance and faith in Jesus Christ.

We deny that the mission of the church is the self-development of exploited peoples or the political liberation of oppressed peoples.[2]

On behalf of one ideal, evangelism, the "DuPage Declaration" speaks to the other two ideals. It also speaks for evangelicals of other denominations, who conjointly drafted and subscribed to it, indicating that the divisions within Methodism are replicated in other "mainline" denominations. It is worth underscoring this point, for both the evangelical/liberal division and the search for a balm to heal it characterize many of the so-called mainline denominations. Indeed, one recent observer has insisted that this division has displaced denominational and confessional differences as the significant fault line in American religious life.[3] Evangelicals from the several denominations feel themselves pulled together, as the "DuPage Declaration" certainly indicates. Liberals enjoy comity through ecumenical activities and working relationships between and among the professionals in the boards and agencies. Essentially the same fissures run through American politics and society. Not a denominationally fragmented Christianity but ideologically rent denominations constitute the present scandal of a divided Christianity.

It may seem naive to hope that the re-imaging offered here would cure these divisions. A Methodist metaphor for thinking about the ideals? Surely a few words and a concept or two can do very little to heal divisions that run so deep. And yet, (1) because it was Christ's wish for his disciples "That ye love one another, as I have loved you," and "That they all may be one; as thou Father, art in me, and I in thee, that they also may be one in us: that the world may believe that thou has sent me";[4] and (2) because unity in mission was a central and motivating concern for John Wesley and early Methodism; and (3) because unity and unity in mission are constitutional and constitutive marks of United Methodists who in the "Preamble" and initial articles to their constitution affirm:

The Church of Jesus Christ exists in and for the world, and its very dividedness is a hindrance to its mission in that world.

As part of the Church Universal, The United Methodist Church believes that the Lord of the Church is calling Christians everywhere to strive toward unity; and therefore it will seek, and work for, unity at all levels of church life . . . .;[5]

and (4) because therefore we live in Christ and in his church under an imperative to search for unity, a few words that evoke important Methodist commitments should not be inappropriate.

The Threefold Problem

Each of the three ideals--justice, evangelism, ecumenism--would present itself as the unitive solution. And even within the General Commission on Christian Unity and Interreligious Concerns (GCCUIC) all three ideals have standing as possible routes to the unity sought.[6]

Justice here will be construed as standing for the unity of the whole creation sought through struggles for "justice, peace and the integrity of creation"[7] and also through the dialogue among and between representatives of the living religions.

Evangelism will stand for the unity sought through missions and witness, bringing unity by the winning of souls to Christ; but it will also stand for the unity within the denomination between those who put such a premium on evangelism and those whose priorities lie elsewhere. This unity concerns the fissures between evangelicals and liberals, with particular attention to the divisions those identities create within Methodism but with obvious import for the lines drawn between those two parties in the larger arenas.

Ecumenism will stand for the unity of Christians, the healing and renewing of Christ's body through the mutual recognition of ministers and members, inclusive eucharistic fellowship and other forms of unity.[8]

The three "ideals" may serve to heal as well as to divide and diagnose. As competing ideals they divide the church; as a complex of assumptions and theory about reality they diagnose the church's situation in the world; as a program, they offer the church a set of solutions. At every level in the connection, the three ideals divide, diagnose, and attempt to heal. What relief can be found for a troubled Zion?

Unifying the Schemes for Unity

The relation and priority among competing ideals of unity is an old and ongoing concern. The *Discipline* in the article cited above proceeds to specify several types of unity in which United Methodism should engage, specifically "world relationships with other Methodist churches," "councils of churches," and "plans of union." It does not indicate precisely how the church might hold those together or put them into priority order. Those tasks have been left to GCCUIC and the Council of Bishops, where discussion does proceed on both the types of unity just mentioned and those delineated by our three ideals. In such discussions, some hold out for a particular type of unity, for energetic participation in World Methodism, bilateral relations or COCU,[9] for instance, to the relative neglect of the others. Other persons insist, as apparently do many within the World Council of Churches and the larger ecumenical arenas, on the interrelated character of the various kinds of unity.

In my own very limited observance of GCCUIC affairs, I have been troubled by such insistence on the seamless quality of ecumenism. I found myself especially perturbed by the enthusiasm lavished on inter-religious dialogue, by the interjection of concern for other religions when items of Christian unity were on the table, and by the commission's efforts to hold together the agendas represented in its name. How, I wondered, would this body really lead the denomination in reception of COCU, due for attention at the next General Conference, if its attention remains so fragmented? With what theological rationale does the commission insist on equating the unity of the Body of Christ to dialogue with other religions? (Why should Methodists, who know that if others' Christian hearts are as our hearts to give them our hands, extend ourselves in the same way for the Muslim or Hindu?) I remained unconvinced that the justice or interreligious agenda, important though it might be, really belonged to Christian unity.

Something of a conversion occurred during a recent conference for United Methodist seminaries under the sponsorship of GCCUIC, the Division of Ordained Ministry, and the Association of United Methodist Theological Schools. What really brought a change of heart was Bishop Roy Sano's insistence that global, interreligious, and ecumenical issues were preeminently local, that rural communities monitor the international economy on which their books balance, and that the opportunities and divisions represented abstractly by terms like "interreligious" manifest themselves immediately and concretely in neighbor and family.[10] During his talk, I made my own inventory and discovered, as I indicated through my opening remarks, that the various kinds of unity do impinge as problem and opportunity in the congregations. With that recognition came the realization that the several types of unity must be held together if the congregation itself is to be held together.

The Three Meals of Methodism

Conversions in both scripture and the history of the church have often been portrayed as eye-opening experiences. While holding that grace undergirds the entire process, Arminians nevertheless believe that some eye-opening precedes the conversion--even as the conversion opens the eyes to the full realities of the human condition. My conversion proceeded in this fashion, impelled by the discovery (from my own research) of a Methodist way of seeing the problem, and also pulled by the realization that some such resolution needed to be found. From Methodist life came a metaphor that made it possible for me to see the several ideals as related and to understand the several kinds of unity as inseparable (though not indistinguishable or necessarily of the same importance). The metaphor derives from that staple of 19th-century Methodist life, the camp meeting.

Three meals sustained the camp meeting: the eucharist, or communion, the love feast, and the family meal. Camp meetings required all three. Communion could be said to have brought the camp meeting into being. The meetings had their spiritual origins in the large-scale sacramental meetings and quarterly conferences that characterized pietism, and particularly Methodism, in the late 18th century.[11] When the stylized camp meeting eventually emerged, it continued to feature the communion service. Also carried over into the camp meeting from the quarterly meeting were the love feasts, that Methodist borrowing from the Moravians, which featured religious testimony sustained through a simple meal of bread and water. Camp meetings were camp meetings because families settled into rustic living on the grounds and therefore made provision for an extended stay. One such provision was eating, and the accounts of camp meetings recall the flickering camp fires as well as the love feasts and eucharists. Camp meetings, at least those under Methodist sponsorship, required all three. They could not exist without the family meal, would have been unthinkable without the love feast, and would have been incomplete without the eucharist.

The family meals, though they divided the camp by kin and by race, were the most inclusive. The unregenerate spouse or child who came grumbling to the occasion (and whose conversion highlights the camp meeting accounts) would have been welcome, indeed, expected at this meal. Here, as it were, the world partook. Slave families at such events rather especially suggest the worldly, even interreligious character of the camp meeting, for their Christianity reverberated with African pulses, and their meals might well have included members whose religiosity remained essentially African. In the family meal, Methodism made table fellowship with the world. It did so uneasily, perhaps testily--one can imagine a wife coaxing her unconverted husband or son over dinner with a firmness that made conviviality impossible and civility the only hope or a teenager lampooning an exhorter who had tripped over his tongue --but there was genuine fellowship nonetheless.

Love feasts would have been the most exclusive, reserved theoretically for Methodist members of society in good standing. Disciplinary rules expressly limited the times that a non-member might observe.[12] These were witnessing occasions. Here a society or circuit divided by some issue--not into today's liberal and conservative but perhaps over the equally explosive matter of slavery--might find renewal and unity. For evangelicals, the love feast returned to the basics--the recounting of conversion experiences and the simple meal, one uniting through the ear and memory, the other through taste, both employing the senses to renew and unite hearts. Love feasts dealt intradenominationally. Only Methodists need appear. The Presbyterian or Baptist at the camp meeting could simply sleep in. Methodists would be up at the crack of dawn for this simple meal, a fellowship well designed to hold the movement together.

Communion could be either inclusive or exclusive depending on who celebrated. Baptists and Presbyterians, who often cooperated with Methodists in staging camp meetings, would reserve communion to their own kind, a behavior paralleling Methodist policy on the love feast. Methodists, on the other hand, offered a more open eucharist.[13] Then, as today, Methodist communion would have welcomed the larger Christian family. "Ye that do truly and earnestly repent of your sins, and are in love and charity with your neighbors . . . ." Though non-Methodists did not always find this invitation compelling, Methodists nevertheless made eucharistic fellowship possible.

In the three camp meeting meals, then, early Methodists stylized the three ideals and the unity possible around each. At the common family table, all members justly received their fare, even though at other tables the family would divide. Justice, equity, decency demanded that the whole family, even the worldly, be fed. In the love feast, Methodists found unity through witness, a table designed for the household of faith. That spiritual intensity fed intradenominational unity and harmony. In communion, Methodists offered a table open to the larger Christian family. The camp meeting required all three meals; it set three tables. Each and all provided sustenance for the camp meeting through which Methodism offered itself to and for the world.[14]

Three Covenants

Although we cannot and should not seek renewal by some repetition of the camp meeting and its meals, we might do well to reflect further on what those meals say about Methodist belief. The three tables call to mind three covenants.[15] Methodists do not typically formalize these covenants theologically in the manner of the Calvinists or always give them the ritual expression they deserve. And yet, Methodists have a clear sense of each, and more importantly, an appreciation of the social bonds and realities which each entails, and at least some realization that they are brought into being and sustained by Christ.

Each table and meal depends upon its particular covenant. The family meal rests on the marriage covenant. The love feast, the missing rite in much of contemporary Methodism, belonged preeminently to the quarterly meeting and to the covenant that Methodists struck with one another. Its constitutional derivative today would be the charge or church conference, an organizational and business affair wanting the joy and intensity of the love feast and rendering the mutuality of that

GLOBALIZATION IN THEOLOGICAL EDUCATION

earlier covenant in fiscal and political terms. Communion, of course, derives from the church covenant, Christ's promise to be with us savingly in that meal.

Though the grace available differs, Christ is not missing from the other meals. The family meal points to the creation, to God's sustaining of the natural order, to the divine ordering of the social and political realms, to the possibility that the common things of life--our meat and drink--might orient us to God's will. This prevenient grace works on and binds together those who do and those who do not call upon Christ's name. So we would understand the marriage covenant as holding together spouses who marry across religious boundaries (as well as families who share the same denomination) and pointing to the grace working throughout the human family.[16] Marriage is a gift to the human family. The grace that sustains it makes possible the good order of the world. It also makes possible a nurturing family life that redounds directly to the church. Hence our preference for a religious rather than civil marriage and for the church's blessing of the bonds that the couple accepts. But we do not typically limit the ceremony to believers, and therefore we do implicitly accept that this covenant belongs to God's larger family. The marriage covenant points especially to God the Father, the Lord of creation.

The love feast points particularly to the Spirit, the Spirit at work in the Methodist faithful, that makes witness possible, that unites and renews, that gives life to the church. In early Methodism, the love feast was routinely celebrated at quarterly conferences and quarterly conferences held in connection with camp meetings. Then the circuit gathered in witness to the commitment that held it together, to a peculiar covenant struck between a preacher and the people who gathered to hear him at preaching stops for four weeks and to the connection that these people had made with one another. The people who attended these powerful gatherings and experiences gave their testimony to the work of the Spirit with bodily expressions and sobbing and shouting. For such self-disclosures, love feasts needed a prior sense of intimacy and confidentiality; they also established it further. The love feast functioned only when it was limited to those who had chosen to travel the Methodist road. Their sanctifying grace was limited to those justified. It is this grace that seems so missing in Methodism, a grace that is wanted to heal the chasm that divides evangelical and liberal, to call Methodists so united to that higher road of Christian perfection that has been our peculiar testimony, and to give vibrance and spirit to our cause.

Communion, on the other hand, Methodists understood and understand as a saving ordinance. In it, Christ is available to those who would orient their lives to receive him. It points to him and joins in covenant all those who call upon his name. Of the meals celebrated at camp meetings, it has been the most fully and faithfully sustained in modern Methodism. Indeed, through the ecumenical liturgical renewal that has shaped our new rites, we have added eucharistic riches to the treasures that we, through Wesley, had derived from the Anglican tradition. Both old and new rites, because they belong really to the wider Christian heritage, point unmistakably to the wider covenant of Christ with his church. And the text and actions make that referent unmistakable.

Feast and Famine

Three meals sustained the camp meeting. Many drew sustenance from all three meals; some partook of two; others would have been permitted only at one. Within United Methodism today we need the grace of all three.

Our family meals should always remind us of those who eat and those who do not eat across the globe, of those who by the common meal are made one even though we do not share a common witness, and of our responsibility to make sure that the bread is broken so that all may eat. We cannot do without our daily bread. In giving thanks for it, we accept in covenant all who share God's created order.[17] The ideal of justice and the unity of creation through justice belongs to us as Methodists.

Nor can we do without communion. By our more frequent celebration, Methodists now recognize how vital this is to our life together. In remaining true to their understanding of communion, Methodists need to proclaim their open table but also to work zealously to make tables genuinely open. Real unity among Christians is our prayer. We must be willing to accept the sacrifices that bring answers to that prayer. As Methodists we should be about the healing and renewing of Christ's body through the mutual recognition of ministers and members, inclusive eucharistic fellowship, and other forms of unity.

We have, unhappily, done without the love feast. The meal that comes closest is the dinner on the grounds or the church potluck. Something of the conviviality of the camp meeting affair survives in such meals, which in a sense links them historically with the camp meeting. But gone are its intimacy and grace. Methodism needs to reclaim this meal and its covenant, for the unitive ideal of evangelism belongs very much to Methodism. But it cannot be the posture of one party. Real evangelical missions by Methodism require the commitment of the whole church. Such unity can come on the terms of neither party, and the posturing by Good News cited above does little to achieve real commitment on the part of the denomination to the ideals for which Good News stands. Unity around the ideal of evangelism, no less than that around the other ideals, is costly, but it is worth the cost so that evangelicals and liberals can eat love feast together.

The meals, families, and covenants need to be held together. And yet the several kinds of unity, though inseparable, are not indistinguishable. And Methodists need to know when and where to eat, how their eating binds them to others, and which dinner invitations take priority. We employ various strategems for dealing with the invitations. Some would accept only one invitation, hold up the banner of only one of the ideals and reject the other two. So, for instance, some believe that justice or evangelism is the United Methodist priority. Others would give priority to one and subsume the other two. A few, particularly in the ecumenical camp, would insist on holding all three together. The latter has been argued here, but with the realization that there will be occasions in which priority does have to be established.

To my own tastes, when invitations force some prioritizing, the ascending order would be family, communion, love feast (justice, ecumenism, evangelism). We obviously cannot do without any. We cannot do without our daily bread. But for eternal well-being, the food of heaven, communion takes priority. When commitments to the two families come into conflict, when the two covenants divide our loyalties, when choice has to be made between interreligious dialogue or Christian unity, the latter has precedence. Similarly, the unity in the Spirit takes highest priority.[18] It does so because it depends upon, presumes and evokes communion, because of what we must attest, because our system does work, because ecumenism is not irrelevant, and because we need to be united so as to share our testimony. I have no misgivings about our zealous pursuit of the next stage in COCU and other such ecumenical ventures. I favor ecumenical explorations by Methodism, as a community confident of its own heritage, of what it brings to the table, of its peculiar grace, of the covenant it enjoys. So also renewal of the Methodist covenant in the Spirit makes genuine dialogue with persons of other faiths and accountability to the needs of the whole creation both possible and imperative. The three meals do belong together; all are, in fact, necessary. Communion really is the basic meal, the one that makes it possible for us to enjoy the other two; the love feast provides a peculiarly Methodist accent to its own life and its involvement in the lives of others.

Notes

1. Here we make the assumption that advocates of any one ideal are unlikely to triumph, thereby producing that model of unity. Unity by victory would probably result in a major division or significant membership losses, depending on whether the losing party or parties exited collectively or individually.

2. *Good News*, 23 (May/June 1990), 41. These points, III and VII, included also affirmations of justification by grace and the imperative of Christian witness and discipleship.

3. Robert Wuthnow, *The Struggle for America's Soul: Evangelicals, Liberals, and Secularism* (Grand Rapids: William B. Eerdmans, 1989) and *The Restructuring of American Religion* (Princeton: Princeton University Press, 1988).

4. John 15:12; 17:21 (KJV). The glory which thou has given me I have given them, that they may be one, even as we are one, I in them, and thou in me, that they may become perfectly one, so that the world may know that thou hast sent me and hast loved them even as thou has loved me" (RSV). See also vv. 22-23:

5. *The Book of Discipline of the United Methodist Church, 1988*. (Nashville: The United Methodist Publishing House, 1988), "Part I. The Constitution: Preamble" and "Division One--General: #5, Article V, Ecumenical Relations" 19, 21. For an illuminating discussion of Christian unity as constitutive of Methodism, see John Deschner, "United Methodism's Ecumenical Policy," *Quarterly Review* 11/3 (Fall 1991): 41-57 (-Chapter 4, "United Methodism's Basic Ecumenical Policy,").

6. The rationale for this threefold schematization of the United Methodist problematic and its resolution will be found below. There are other and more conventional ways of outlining the vying priorities and conceptions of the unity to be sought. For instance, the Center for Ecumenical Dialogue in Longwood, Florida, orders its work into three dialogues--with the Christian Community, with the Religious Community, and with the Human Community--thus distinguishing in its first two dialogues what we have combined in our first. The Center subsumes our second under its first. Our threefold delineation indicates an explicit concern with the disunity within denominations and not incidentally sets up the Methodist metaphor which is the burden of the paper. The proof is, we hope, in the pudding; we beg the reader's patience in its preparation here.

7. This is the title of one of the World Council of Churches processes, a World Convocation for which met in Seoul, Korea, in March 1990. Efforts to tie this concern to faith and order are being carried on through a formal study project entitled "The Unity of the Church and the Renewal of Human Community."

8. Observers of GCCUIC and of United Methodist ecumenical endeavor will recognize the first and third as not only appropriately assigned to, indeed mandated of, GCCUIC, but as embodied in its very name. The middle conception will seem less clearly GCCUIC's. The recognition by that agency of the unity within the denomination can be seen in its recent efforts to work more effectively with the World Methodist Council, in attention within its meetings to the larger agenda of conversations with the church's evangelical wing and

in an effectively sounded call by Bishop Roy Sano to work toward that end. For the latter, see Roy I. Sano, "Ecumenical and Interreligious Agenda of the United Methodist Church," Quarterly Review 11/1 (Spring 1991): 82-97.

9. The acronym will be probably more familiar than the phrase for which it now stands, "The Church of Christ Uniting." Its older referent was for "Consultation on Church Union," the structure and process which has recently produced a new covenanting proposal now before the denominations for action. For particulars, see the two descriptive documents, The COCU Consensus: In Quest of a Church of Christ Uniting, ed. Gerald F. Moede (Princeton: COCU, 1985) and Churches in Covenant Communion: The Church of Christ Uniting (Princeton: COCU, 1989) (- Chapter 3, "The Local Church and the World: Ecumenical and Interreligious Agenda of The United Methodist Church,").

10. "Ecumenical and Interreligious Agenda of the United Methodist Church," pp. 85-88.

11. See my "From Quarterly to Camp Meeting," Methodist History 23 (July, 1985), 199-213, and Kenneth O. Brown, "Finding America's Oldest Camp Meeting," Methodist History 28 (July 1990), 252-54, and Charles A. Johnson, The Frontier Camp Meeting (Dallas: Southern Methodist University Press, 1955).

12. The first Discipline queried: "How often shall we permit strangers to be present at our love feasts?" and stipulated "Ans. Let them be admitted with the utmost caution; and the same person on no account above twice, unless he becomes a member." The first Discipline and Large Minutes are conveniently compared in History of the Discipline of the Methodist Episcopal Church by Robert Emory, rev. W.P. Strickland (New York: Carlton & Porter, [1857?]). See p. 29.

13. The first Discipline specified a controlled invitation: "Let no person who is not a member of the society be admitted to the communion, without a sacrament ticket, which ticket must be changed every quarter. And we em - power the elder or assistant, and no others, to deliver these tickets." Emory, History of the Discipline, 45.

14. We have not attempted here to treat the camp meeting as a whole and so therefore slight the other offices, particularly preaching, that played such an important role in Methodism's spreading scriptural holiness over the land and reforming the continent. The point of this essay is not to propose the modality of Methodism's engagement with the world or even the means by which unity might be achieved. Were we to do so certainly other means of grace would take more prominence and preaching would receive its due. The point rather is to discover how, as Methodism went about its work, it managed to hold itself together.

15. I use the present rather than the past tense here to indicate that, in subjecting this metaphor to theological attention, we are proceeding beyond what early Methodism verbalized about the camp meetings. It is my conviction, elaborated in other essays, that early Methodist theology was a theology of action, structure, and ritual. It needs to be exhibited in its fullness and respected for its texture. But then the action, structure or ritual needs also to

be analyzed if we would understand what Methodists believed. For their "thought" or theology was embedded in the forms by which Methodism lived. Of no event is this more true than the camp meeting. Methodists then and thereafter knew that it said something very important about themselves. But they found no good way of elaborating what it said, except by performing it. Their orthopraxy requires theological analysis from us if we would do them justice. Hence here we will speak of the meals and covenants as 20th-century Methodist possibilities. This presumes, of course, that that earlier practice might be instructive to us today. I do not intend to suggest that we ought to reinstitute the camp meeting. I am suggesting that we reclaim the three meals.

16. By limiting marriage within the faith community, some traditions and most sectarian movements place the marriage or family covenant within the church covenant. The more expansive notion outlined here would seem more in keeping with Methodist thought.

17. Even our meals around the TV, though they rob the nourishment that we give each other, mediate the world to us and thus point to this larger covenant. Obviously, the TV dinner would need some creative attention and interpretation before it could function in this way.

18. It is important to underscore the point that love feast can have priority only insofar as it always depends upon and points to communion. We do not here intend to undo the Reformation and establish another sacrament or in any way diminish the Eucharist. Rather, we would reclaim the distinctive Methodist commitment to perfection, wholeness, and sanctification. We understand that this higher life is always fueled by the grace of baptism and communion but nevertheless aspires to the fullness of Christ-like existence that baptism and communion make possible. The love feast symbolizes that fullness. It is worth recovering.

THE LOCAL CHURCH AND THE WORLD:

Ecumenical and Interreligious Agenda of The United Methodist Church

ROY I. SANO

When we speak of the ecumenical and interreligious agenda of The United Methodist Church, our attention is directed to the future. An "agenda" suggests topics requiring further exploration and discussion. I would like to look to the past, however, for clues concerning the unfinished agenda we must address in the days ahead.

The United Methodist Church's vast involvement in ecumenical and interreligious ventures in recent decades and in the present is a convenient place to begin. In these pages I can only offer an abbreviated listing of the major types of ecumenical and interreligious efforts. But I will use this sampling as a basis to explore the ecumenical agenda for The United Methodist Church (UMC) and its implications for theological education.

Involvements

Our commitments to ecumenism and interreligious efforts are substantial. I turn first to the ecumenical ventures. In the Uniting Conference of UMC in 1968, the denomination adopted a statement, "On the Ecumenical Road."[1] At the same General Conference the denomination also wrote into The Constitution of the United Methodist *Discipline* the following mandate:

As part of the Church Universal, The United Methodist Church believes that the Lord of the Church is calling Christians everywhere to strive toward unity; and therefore it will seek, and work for, unity at all levels of church life: through world relationships with other Methodist churches and united churches related to The Methodist Church or The Evangelical United Brethren Church, through councils of churches, and through plans of union with churches of Methodist or other denominations.[2]

The passage suggests three basic types of ecumenical relationships and ventures. Under each type I will cite examples. First, the mandate mentions direct relationships which we have as a denomination with other Methodist Churches or united churches related to our predecessor denominations. We make provisions for direct relationships through affiliations, concordats, and covenants with autonomous Methodist churches.[3] Such ties exist, for example, with the British Methodists. Dialogues and consultations with other churches might be mentioned in this connection though not explicitly mandated in the constitutional provision. We have pursued bilateral dialogues, for example, with Roman Catholics[4] and with Lutheran denominations.[5] We have also joined other denomination in ministries and mission, such as in disaster relief.[6]

If the first type of unity establishes relationships directly with other denominations, the second pursues these relationships indirectly, through councils of churches. The World Methodist Council can be mentioned in this connection,[7] as can the World Council of Churches[8] and the National Council of the Churches of Christ in the USA.[9]

Third, we have pursued plans of union with churches of Methodist or other denominational traditions. We have participated, for example, in the Consultation on Church Union since its beginning in 1961.[10]

I turn now from ecumenical ventures to interreligious efforts. The denomination does not have a constitutional mandate for interreligious pursuits comparable to the statement on "Ecumenical Relations." There are, nevertheless, official denominational statements adopted by the General Conference. In 1972 the church adopted the statement, "Bridge in Hope: Jewish-Christian Dialogue."[11] In 1980, the church issued a statement, "Called to be Neighbors and Witnesses: Guidelines for Interreligious Relationships,"[12] affirming the place of witness and dialogue.

Although it is not constitutional, an important official statement appears in the *1988 Discipline* in the section entitled "Our Theological Task." Ecumenism is used broadly in this setting.

Concurrently, we have entered into serious interfaith encounters and explorations between Christians and adherents of other living faiths of the world. Scripture calls us to be both neighbors and witnesses to all people. Such encounters require us to reflect anew on our faith and seek guidance for our witness among neighbors of other faiths.[13]

In line with these observations, the denomination, acting through the General Commission on Christian Unity and Interreligious Concerns (GCCUIC), has continued interreligious dialogues, for example, with

Muslims and adherents of American Indian spirituality. The results of these interactions can be found in minutes and reports. As of this moment these dialogues have not produced official stands. United Methodism's participation in numerous interreligious ventures through the WCC also should be mentioned in this connection.[14]

While this summary of ecumenical and interreligious efforts is succinct, each example can be compared to a central switchboard at the twin towers of the World Trade Center in New York. One connection branches off into innumerable relationships and ventures. It should be clear, therefore, why no attempt to summarize these activities can ever be complete.[15]

Appropriating the Contributions

1. Local Churches

The contributions of ecumenical and interreligious efforts must be tied into the life of our local congregations, and it is the role of theological seminaries to train persons to do so.

We must overcome two stereotypes if we are to recognize the potential contributions of our ecumenical and interreligious efforts. One has to do with our picture of our people in local churches; the other has to do with the nature of ecumenical proposals and their use.

When local congregations object to ecumenical proposals and interreligious dialogue, there is often media coverage of their protest. This gives a false impression of the local congregation. We consequently overlook the interdenominational composition of the membership and their awareness of the global context in which they live out their lives--the very qualities that create a readiness to receive[16] the contributions of ecumenical ventures and interreligious dialogues.

Our membership is increasingly interdenominational. In growing numbers of local congregations, up to two-thirds of the membership come from other denominations. Even where the upbringing of members is still predominately United Methodist, denominational loyalties mean much less. As we will discuss below, there is even animus against denominational interests by certain special interest groups who appeal to a Wesleyan heritage.[17]

Furthermore, the experiences of our people are much more cosmopolitan--and therefore imbued with more interreligious qualities--than we generally recognize. Recently I heard that one travel agent in Bozeman, Montana (population: 25,000) supports herself on the travel arrangements for six families. Imagine the impact of such frequent travel on these families and those who work for them on their ranches and farms.

Many farmers in the plains states listen to the price of their grains on the world market before leaving home for work at 5:30 in the morning. They listen to international news as they ride in the air-conditioned cabs of their combines. These farmers can visualize their grain moving across interstate truck routes and train tracks in the U.S. They are familiar with the shipping lanes connecting major ports which send their products around the globe. Agriculturalists in America's heartland are hardly parochial and uninformed about the global networks in which they live and work.

The global economic consciousness fostered by their livelihood creates a climate of understanding for the interfaith dialogues that cross national and cultural boundaries. Economic relationships across the Pacific Basin, for example, are influenced by Confucianism and Buddhism, whose roots are deep in Asian and Pacific cultures. Church members in these areas experience economic rivalries and cultural clashes in varying ways each year. All too often, their pastors are ill-equipped to deal with the interreligious aspects of these problems.

Because our members are far more interdenominational and their experiences touched with interreligious exchanges in their daily life, I have often found that ecumenical and interfaith documents bear directly on the life of our congregations and their experiences in the world. An analogy from stewardship will explain how the results of ecumenical and interreligious dialogues can be used in local churches. The beginning point in cultivating stewardship is to affirm the great things our members are already doing with God and God's people. Even if their gifts are minimal, we can still have much to celebrate. This affirmation and celebration must precede any new challenges and additional responsibilities we place before our members.

The same point applies to our stands and proposals in ecumenical and interreligious pursuits. They can help us understand the ecumenical experiences and interreligious exchanges already occurring in and among our people. Like the work of a great artist, ecumenical convergences and analyses of interreligious dialogues help us look at everyday occurrences with new eyes. That is, the documents help us describe or name what is already experienced and occurring among our people.

Two concrete examples will suffice. We can treat the World Council of Church's seminal document, *Baptism, Eucharist and Ministry* (BEM), as a highly abbreviated summary of erudite biblical scholars, church historians, theologians, and liturgical scholars.[18] In point of fact, however, since 1972 our congregations have increasingly used over twenty alternate worship resources that incorporated the emerging convergence which produced BEM. The final edition of BEM in 1982, therefore, describes to a considerable extent what many churches were already experiencing but had not articulated for themselves. BEM should not be portrayed as something wholly new to our congregations or unrelated to their experiences.

Consider further the process of covenanting that we have developed as members of the Consultation on Church Union (COCU). Members in local churches are already taking a good number of the steps proposed in *Churches in Covenant Communion: The Church of Christ Uniting.* As laypeople move freely across denominational lines, they are experiencing considerable unity in faith. They recognize one another's baptism and acknowledge various denominations as expressions of Christ's true church. Many of our laity welcome the ordained ministries of other communions. They experience the presence of Christ and proclaim his Parousia in various services of the Lord's Supper. These documents describe the best that people already practice and appreciate, as well as the trajectories that their life in Christ will continue to take.

Of course, there are those who resist ecumenical statements, but this is often a reaction to those who promote ecumenism. In their zeal, these persons suggest that their products are avant-garde, perhaps even radical and revolutionary, and that church members are benighted and backward. Their condescending tone speaks louder than the substance of the achievement. It is little wonder that after decades of this abuse, some longsuffering parishioners have begun to protest. The irony is that such ecumania is decidedly un-ecumenical! If we are to realize the great gains we have made for Christian unity and interfaith relations, it will be necessary to move beyond these stereotypes of local churches and adopt new approaches.

2. Theological Seminaries

If theological seminaries are to train persons to fully appropriate ecumenical and interreligious gains in recent decades, there is much work to be done. To begin with, library resources and faculty skills in interreligious dialogue are growing rapidly. We can celebrate this fact. Comparable resources for Christian unity, however, are lagging considerably. Only the exceptional library has the documentation on one commission in the World Methodist Council[19] or the World Council of Churches.[20] Records of dialogues between and among churches on significant issues are generally absent in library holdings. It is no wonder that these resources are hardly ever introduced as instructive insights for interpreting human experiences.[21]

In one sense, these oversights are understandable. Ecumenical documents, which are often brief statements, represent a new and distinct literary genre. Learning how to read some of them is like learning an ancient ceremonial language. These brief statements compress days, weeks, months, and even years of intense discussion, but their slight appearance seems to encourage facile dismissals. This is evidently the case in theological education, for faculty members seldom find occasion to consult such documents or request libraries to acquire them.

Such neglect is unfortunate to say the least. Church leaders who ignore resources that interpret the church in its local, regional, and global dimensions are like economists who ignore key economic forces in society. Can we imagine a library or faculty members at a university department in economics overlooking labor unions, small businesses, multinational corporations, and governmental and nongovernmental agencies interacting with them? Many people in the church already charge seminaries with an ivory tower mentality, saying that they overlook the very institutions through which religious forces act most immediately and directly. Many religious leaders turn to centers for congregational studies; the Rollins Center in Atlanta or the Alban Institute are cases in point. Theological educators who look at the products of the ecumenical and interreligious ventures, however, can uncover the dynamics of local churches, regional bodies, and in global church networks.

Theological seminaries must acquire the resources and train persons in the use of these documents. To repeat, the fruits of the ecumenical and interreligious ventures help us see what we are already experiencing but had not noticed. As with Christian faith itself, we first "believe in order to understand." In seeing our experiences and actions more clearly, we can then use our insights to plan better steps ahead.

My second general line of exploration moves from contributions to corrective, from complimenting what ecumenical and interreligious leaders offer us to complementing or supplementing their contributions.

Pursuing New Directions

1. Broadening the Scope

Based on my summary of United Methodist involvements in ecumenism and interreligious dialogue, there are two directions I would suggest. First, we should continue to broaden the scope of ecumenical and interreligious efforts at several points, particularly in our efforts in relations with our Jewish, Muslim, and Native American neighbors. Each requires additional work. We must also consider relations with persons whose primary religious influence is Hinduism, Buddhism, Confucianism, Taoism, and Shintoism. These Asian traditions are vital for over half of humankind. In our interactions with persons around the globe, animism surely is of major significance for our neighbors in Latin America, Africa, Asia, and the islands of the seas.

To understand these living traditions, we must use methods for study and interaction that move beyond those based solely on the European Renaissance and Enlightenment. In both eras, the major approach was literary. While the verbal products of any civilization are surely among its richest expressions, people express themselves in more than simply literary texts. We need the analytical tools and procedures associated with cultural anthropology to interpret symbolic interactions or artistic artifacts in music and dance, mime and drama, paintings and architecture, clothes and food.[22] The same can be said for social psychology[23] and political economy.[24]

With reference to political economy, we owe COCU a word of gratitude for including a section entitled "Commitment to Seek Unity with Wholeness" in its proposal, *Churches in Covenant Communion: The Church of Christ Uniting.*[25] Ever since the 1975 plenary session, COCU has issued "alerts" concerning the "new church-dividing potentials of some persisting issues." These factors were distinguished from the explicitly stated doctrinal points of contention.[26] Such an approach is certainly valid. Our own history reminds us of the role that slavery played in the division of our predecessor denomination. Racism continues to haunt us, and that is why I suggest that we narrow the scope of our agenda as well.

2. Narrowing the Scope

While much of our most prominent efforts in ecumenism have been interdenominational and interreligious, we now face a need to be intradenominational as well. We must focus, therefore, on evangelical and liberal tensions and conflicts. Robert Wuthnow, a sociologist of religion at Princeton University, has described it well:

Polarization...has come to characterize American religion--the deep cultural divide between conservative or evangelical Christians, on the one side, and religious liberals and secular humanists, on the other side. According to public opinion polls, this cleavage is fraught with considerable misgiving and stereotyping on both sides. It divides the nation into two opposing camps that are approximately equal in numbers, and it cuts directly through most of the nation's major denominational families and faith traditions.[27]

The United Methodist Church has virtually two parallel denominations within the existing one. Conservative evangelicals have developed their own seminary and publishing house, their own boards of global ministries and church and society, their own network of evangelism and education, and much more. If it had not been for the pension program and the trust clause, which prohibits removal of property to another denomination by "local option," we could very well have split the denomination several years ago.

I direct our attention to this reality because of our history. The nineteenth century holiness movement in the Wesleyan household eventually became a divisive force and produced a proliferation of denominations. The emergence of the holiness groups represented what Nathan O. Hatch has called "the democratization of American Christianity"[28] amidst what Alice Felt Tyler called "freedom's ferment."[29] The existing denomination could not incorporate the new burst of energies because of its narrow liturgical practices, theology, and missional outreach. The new movements therefore were forced to leave and organize a new denomination.

In a diversified denomination, the conservative evangelical Wesleyans are now asking us to acknowledge our distinctly white heritage as much as we have highlighted the contributions of people of color. They are asking us to affirm the contributions of males as much as we have highlighted the contributions of women. It does not surprise us that evangelicals appeal to John Wesley, a white male Anglo-Saxon.

While many factors are operating in the resurgence of conservative, Wesleyan evangelicalism in the United Methodist Church, we cannot overlook the ethnic factor. This sector of the church lost patience waiting for an affirmative word about white people in this nation and have therefore launched a patriotic campaign. In his analysis of the "New Right" in American politics in the 1980s, Alan Crawford spoke of a "resentment" lying at the heart of the conservative movement.[30] Conservatives have taken it upon themselves to oppose those progressives who say how evil and wrong the U.S. has been. They long to hear a witness of the Spirit (Rom. 8:16) that they too are "children of God" and not simply the scourge of the earth that liberals at home and people of color around the world seem to say that they are.

The intradenominational ecumenical agenda therefore calls for new ways to affirm and celebrate diversity. We must be inclusive of whites as well as people of color; men as much as women; straights as much as persons with alternate lifestyles; and ordinary people as well as special people with handicapping conditions. Unless we find ways of incorporating this heritage more explicitly in our theology and ethics, alienation will grow among conservative evangelicals and schism becomes a greater probability.

What does inclusivity mean for so-called mainline denominations with a vocal and politically mobilized evangelical movement? This can be determined only through dialogue and experimentation. An ecumenism that is exclusively denominational and neglects the intradenominational tensions between evangelicals and liberals is simply outdated. Unless we take up the ecumenical task within our own denomination, we poison the balm that can heal both divisions within the Body of Christ, and interfaith rivalries in the body politic.

Notes

1. "On the Ecumenical Road: The United Methodist Church and the Cause of Christian Unity," Service Center, Cincinnati, Ohio,13th printing, June, 1986. Items distributed by the Service Center, 7810 Reading Road, Caller No. 1800, Cincinnati, Ohio 45222-1800.

2. *The Book of Discipline of The United Methodist Church, 1988*, (Nashville: The United Methodist Publishing House, 1988), par. 5. Hereafter *Discipline*, with numbers indicating paragraphs and not pagination unless otherwise noted.

It may be important to recall the status of this constitutional commitment to ecumenical relations. Unlike many other portions of the *Discipline* which require a simple majority of General Conference delegates voting, amendments to this portion of The Constitution only occur with "two thirds present and voting and a two thirds affirmative vote of the aggregate number of members of the several Annual Conferences present and voting."(62).

3. *Discipline*, 647-654.

4. The UMC-Roman Catholic Dialogues have produced three documents. The first round produced an agreement on "Holiness and Spirituality of the Ordained Ministry: A Report of The United Methodist-Roman Catholic Dialogue 1976," which is available from the Publication Office, United States Catholic Conference, 1312 Massachusetts Avenue, NW, Washington, D.C. 20005. The second dialogue from the 1977-81 which produced "Eucharistic Celebration: Converging Theology--Diverging Practice" is now out of print. Participants in a third dialogue issued "Holy Living and Holy Dying: A United Methodist/Roman Catholic Common Statement" (n.d. Stock #1287), available from the Service Center.

This end note and those which follow in this section will list a highly selective sampling, with primary attention to faith and order interests. The sampling will illustrate a point made later in the paper concerning the vast ranging bibliographical resources in ecumenism which theological libraries could consider.

5. The results of the first series of dialogues between UMC and Lutherans between 1977 and 1979 on baptism appear in a special issue of the *Perkins Journal* (34:1981). The second series between 1985-87 produced a statement on "Episcopacy: Lutheran/United Methodist Common Statement to the Church" (Stock #5022), Service Center.

6. See the history in Norman Kehrberg's *Love in Action: UMCOR--50 Years of Service* (Nashville: Abingdon, 1989).

7. *World Methodist Council: Handbook of Information, 1987-1991* (Ashland, N.C.: Biltmore Press, 1987) provides a brief survey of the Council. The *Handbook* is available from the Council office, P.O. Box 518, Lake Junaluska, NC 28745. See the *Proceedings of the Fifteenth World Methodist Council, Nairobi, Kenya, July 23-29, 1986*, edited by Joe Hale (Waynesville, North Carolina: World Methodist Council, 1986) for an indication of the denominational relationship through this "confessional" body (pp. 336-37). The proceedings for the 16th Council meeting July 24-31, 1991, in Singapore, are forthcoming.

Interactions among the various Methodist denominations who are members of the council produced several statements published in the *1986 Proceedings*, including "The North/South Dialogue and Solidarity with the Poor"; the "World Methodist Social Affirmation"; and "Six Major Issues as Methodists Witness to the Gospel."

Documents from dialogues with other world-wide confessional bodies through the World Methodist Council also appear in the *1986 Proceedings*. They include dialogues with the World Alliance of Reformed Churches (1985) on the gospel (pp. 339-42); with the Lutheran World Federation (1979-84) on "The Church: Community of Grace" (pp. 341-60); and with the Roman Catholic Church (fourth series, 1982-85) on the topic, "Toward a Statement on the Church" (pp. 360-72).

The *1986 Proceedings* also mentions the first series of dialogues between the UMC and Roman Catholics. The summary statement appears in *The Denver Report* covering the 1967-70 dialogues on Christianity in the contemporary world, spirituality, family, eucharist, ministry, and authority. The second dialogue appears in *The Dublin Report* covering the 1972-75 period on the eucharist and ordained ministry. The third dialogue appears in *The Honolulu Report* covering the period of 1977-81 on ethical decisions and other topics. All three documents are conveniently found in *Growth in Agreement: Reports and Agreed Statements of Ecumenical Conversations on a World Level, Ecumenical Documents II*, edited by Harding Meyer and Lukas Vischer (New York: Paulist Press, 1984), pp. 307-87. The first two dialogues are summarized in *Confessions in Dialogue: A Study of Bilateral Conversations among World Confessional Families, 1959-1974*, Third, Revised and Enlarged Edition, edited by Nils Ehrenstrom (Geneva: WCC, 1975), pp. 40-44.

8. *Introducing the World Council of Churches* (Geneva: WCC, 1990) by Marlin VanElderen provides a brief orientation to the WCC, including its recent history, current structures, and extensive programs prior to the 7th WCC Assembly in Canberra, 1991. The proceedings of the Assembly are forthcom-

ing. A fuller survey of the efforts appears in *Vancouver to Canberra, 1983-1990, Report of the Central Committee of the World Council of Churches to the Seventh Assembly*, edited by Thomas F. Best (Geneva: WCC, 1990). *The Dictionary of the Ecumenical Movement*, edited by Nicholas Lossky, et al. (Grand Rapids: Wm B. Eerdmans, 1991) includes extensive coverage of the WCC. See the *Handbook: Member Churches, World Council of Churches*, Second Edition edited by Ans J. van der Bent (Geneva: WCC, 1985), for a description of over 300 member churches with which United Methodism has ties through the WCC. *WCC Publications, 1991: Books, Periodicals and Audio-Visuals from the World Council of Churches* can be treated as an annotated bibliography for WCC resources. The catalogue is available from the WCC Distribution Center, P.O. Box 346, Route 222 & Sharadan Road, Kutztown, PA 19530-0346.

Three items will illustrate the immense variety of significant documents produced through the Council of Churches. All three are edited by Ans J. van der Bent. They include *Six Hundred Ecumenical Consultations, 1948-1982* (Geneva: WCC, 1983), *A Guide to Essential Ecumenical Reading* (Geneva: WCC, 1984) and *Vital Ecumenical Concerns* (Geneva: WCC, 1986). An additional volume, *Index to the World Council of Churches' Official Statements and Reports, 1948-1978*, edited by P. Beffa, et al. (Geneva: WCC, 1978) organizes these documents by topic and refers to the volumes in which they appear.

The responses to *Baptism, Eucharist & Ministry* (Geneva: World Council of Churches, 1982) illustrate the enormous volume of documentation from one WCC unit on a single topic having to do with ecumenical relations among Christian churches. See *Ecumenical Perspectives on Baptism, Eucharist and Ministry*, edited by Max Thurian (Geneva: WCC, 1983) for important essays on the document and the follow-up, *Baptism and Eucharist: Ecumenical Convergence in Celebration*, edited by Max Thurian and Geoffrey Wainwright (Geneva: WCC, 1983) for sample liturgies that demonstrate the amazing convergences. As of the writing of this paper, the denominational responses to BEM appear in six volumes of *Churches Respond to BEM: Official Responses to the "Baptism, Eucharist and Ministry" Text* (Geneva: WCC), Volumes 1 and 2, 1986; Volumes 3 and 4, 1987; Volumes 5 and 6, 1988; Volume 7 (1990). See n. 14 below for a sampling of WCC documents related to the second focus on interreligious dialogue at the Yahara Consultation.

9. A sampling of the statements issued from one unit, The Commission on Faith and Order (COFO) of the NCCC, appears in the list of publications in "Program of Studies, 1988-1991," published by COFO/NCCC, 175 Riverside Drive, Room 872, New York, NY 10115-0050.

10. The two most immediately relevant items from COCU are *The COCU Consensus: In Quest of a Church of Christ Uniting*, edited by Gerald F. Moede (Princeton, N.J.: COCU, 1985); and *Churches in Covenant Communion: The Church of Christ Uniting* (Princeton, NJ: COCU, 1989), both available from COCU, Research Park, 151 Wall Street, Princeton, NJ 08540-1514.

11. "Bridge in Hope: Jewish-Christian Dialogue," 7th printing (Cincinnati: Service Center, 1985), #2574.

12. "Called to be Neighbors and Witnesses: Guidelines for Interreligious Relationships," (Cincinnati: Service Center, 1981), #3840.

13. *Discipline*, par. 69 (pp. 88-89).

14. See *Six Hundred Ecumenical Consultations, 1948-1982*, pp. 59-66 for a description of the consultations staged by the WCC on Dialogue with People of Living Faiths and Ideologies and the documents which they produced.

Additional publications include *Guidelines on Dialogues with People of Living Faiths and Ideologies* (Geneva: WCC, 1984); S. Wesley Ariarajah, *The Bible and People of Other Faiths* (Maryknoll, NY: Orbis, 1989); S. J. Smartha, *Courage for Dialogue* (Maryknoll, NY: Orbis, 1981); Tosh Arai and S. Wesley Ariarajah, *Spirituality in Interfaith Dialogues: Testimonies* (Geneva: WCC, 1988); and M. M. Thomas, *Risking Christ for Christ's Sake: Towards an Ecumenical Theology of Pluralism* (Geneva: WCC, 1987).

15. The citations above offer illustrations of the enormous network of ties and joint efforts connected to a single ecumenical or interreligious relationship. References have cited documents primarily related to faith and order dialogues in interreligious concerns. The citations illustrate a point concerning library resources that we will highlight below.

16. *Baptism, Eucharist and Ministry* called for a "process of reception" (p. x). The concept was chosen carefully. Those who selected the word had in mind something akin to the passage in John 1:12: "all who receive [Jesus], who believe in his name, [God] gave power to become children of God." See Ulrich Kuhn, "Reception--An Imperative and an Opportunity," in *Ecumenical Perspectives on Baptism, Eucharist, and Ministry*, pp. 165-68, for the biblical and theological understanding of "reception" drawn from the Greek word *lambanein* and its cognates. See too, Anton Houtepen, "Reception, Tradition, Communion," *ibid.*, pp. 144-49, for its historical usages.

17. See, for example, Robert Wuthnow's observations concerning the declining significance of denominationalism and the growth of special purpose groups in *The Restructuring of American Religion* (Princeton: Princeton University Press, 1988), pp. 71-131. Hence, ecumenical statements are relevant to inter-actions within our membership and not only the relations between denomina-tions at the highest levels.

18. *Baptism, Eucharist & Ministry* (Geneva: World Council of Churches, 1982), Faith and Order Paper No. 111. The extensive work and rich resources related to BEM are described in *Baptism, Eucharist & Ministry, 1982-1990: A Report on the Process and Responses* (Geneva: WCC, 1990).

The 6th WCC Assembly in Vancouver, 1983, at which time the WCC adopted the BEM report, dramatically demonstrated the crucial role of spirituality in the quest for unity in faith, witness, and service. The 6th Assembly has been called the "praying Assembly." Worship resources for the event appeared in *"Jesus Christ--the Life of the World": A Worship Book for the Sixth Assembly of the World Council of Churches* (Geneva: WCC, 1983). Similarly, for the 7th Assembly in Canberra, 1991, the WCC issued *In Spirit and in Truth: A Worship Book* (Geneva: WCC, 1991). Two additional WCC resources for ecumenical prayer and spirituality should be mentioned. *With All God's People: The New Ecumenical Prayer Cycle* (Geneva: WCC, 1989) surveys world Christianity in the contemporary world while offering prayers which are often indigenous to those places. *With All God's People: Orders of Service* (Geneva: WCC, 1989) has drawn together worship services for various settings from member churches. Resources in both volumes were compiled by John Carden.

19. See above, note 7.

20. See above, note 8.

21. See above, notes 4 and 5.

22. Part of D. T. Suzuki's contribution in uncovering the identity and behavior of Japanese people was his combination of careful studies of religious texts with analyses of their social and aesthetic expressions. See, for example, his classic work, *Zen and Japanese Culture* (Princeton: Princeton University Press, 1959). Other analyses might be cited in this connection. *The Chrysanthemum and the Sword: Patterns of Japanese Culture* (New York: World, 1946), by cultural anthopologist Ruth Benedict, also has enduring value. Much of Benedict's field work was conducted among Japanese Americans in the U.S. A more recent example appears from the cultural anthropologists Chie Nakano in her study, *Japanese Society* (Berkeley: University of California Press, 1970). While her work concentrates on Japanese living in Japan, many of her insights bear on Japanese Americans in the U.S.

23. Takeo Doi, *The Anatomy of Dependence*, translated by John Bester (Tokyo: Kodansha International Ltd., 1973) illustrated the usefulness of social psychology with sensitivities to religious heritage of a people. See too, David K. Reynolds, *Morita Psychotherapy* (Berkeley: University of California Press, 1976). John Berthrong, a faculty member of the School of Theology, Boston University, has called my attention to recent studies in Japanese Confucianism and its role in Japanese behavior, including their activities in global economic ventures. He also cites resources which uncover the Confucianist elements in the interactions between Japan and the U.S. in world trade. See Herman Ooms, *Tokugawa Ideology: Early Constructs, 1570-1680* (Princeton: Princeton University Press, 1985); Peter Nosco, ed., *Confucianism and Tokugawa Culture* (Princeton: Princeton University Press, 1984); Tetsuo Nagita, *Visions of Spiritual Cultivation in Japanese Neo-Confucianism: The Life and Thought of Kaibara Ekken (1630-1714)*, (Albany: SUNY Press, 1989).

24. Max Weber's *The Protestant Ethic and the Spirit of Capitalism*, translated by Talcott Parsons (New York: Scribners, 1958), represents a historic example, as does *The Religion of China: Confucianism and Taoism*, translated by Hans A. Gerth (New York: Free Press, 1951). Robert Bellah's *Tokugawa Religion: The Values of Preindustrial Japan* (New York: Macmillan, 1957) traces the religious roots of an emerging political economy which still has implications for understanding Japan. In his landmark work, *God the Economist: The Doctrine of God and Political Economy* (Philadelphia: Fortress, 1989), M. Douglas Meeks provides an example of interpreting the religious dimensions of our own society through its economics.

25. *Churches in Covenant Communion*, pp. 16-18.

26. H. Richard Niebuhr, *The Social Sources of Denominationalism* (New York: Macmillan, 1934). COCU named racism, sexism, institutionalism, and congregational exclusiveness as the chief divisive elements of society. This is a bold statement of the theological foundations for unity in the Body of Christ.

27. Robert Wuthow, *The Struggle for America's Soul: Evangelicals, Liberals, and Secularism* (Grand Rapids: William B. Eerdmans, 1989), p. 17.

28. Nathan O. Hatch, *The Democratization of American Christianity* (New Haven: Yale University Press, 1989).

29. Alice Felt Tyler, *Freedom's Ferment* (Minneapolis: University of Minnesota Press, 1944).

30. Alan Crawford, *Thunder on the Right: The "New Right" and the Politics of Resentment* (New York: Pantheon Books, 1980).

UNITED METHODISM'S BASIC ECUMENICAL POLICY

JOHN DESCHNER

"We are becoming the Sancho Panza of the ecumenical movement," a United Methodist of my acquaintance remarked to me recently. I laughed until it began to sink in. Sancho Panza was the great realist who wept over Don Quixote's windmills; the eternal survivor who made sure there was a next meal, if not a believable future; the faithful follower, seldom the initiator; the man with an absolutely impenetrable tin ear, who lacked even a trace of his master's soaring imagination.

That ecumenical Sancho needs a vision of his own. Not a triumphal Quixote-like vision, but a realistic vision that suits him--a basic ecumenical policy that does for the United Methodist Church what sound basic foreign policy can do for the nation. This paper aims to provoke something like that by clarifying the importance of United Methodism's ecumenical commitment for its health as a church.

Its main affirmations are these: First: Our ecumenical commitment is not an extra, but is essential and constitutive for United Methodism as church.

Second: An adequate basic ecumenical policy for United Methodism will focus upon four points:

1. The central ecumenical goal is an *inclusive church unity as a witness* to God's way of healing and renewing the broken human community.

2. The attainable sign of integrity in that witness is an inclusive, visible *fellowship around the table* in Holy Communion--a fellowship presently not expressed by the divided churches.

3. The unavoidable immediate step toward that witness is: working toward a full inclusive and *mutual recognition of members and ministers* among the divided churches.

4. The historical embodiment of this attainable goal is best viewed as a future truly *ecumenical conciliar event* of witness.

United Methodism's Ecumenical Commitment and Principles

Let's begin constitutionally. How much do United Methodists care about ecumenism? If ecumenism means church unity and its witness concerning the healing and wholeness of human community, then constitutionally United Methodists put that concern right at the top of their self-understanding as a church.

Our Constitution begins with church unity as a witness about human community. It takes the Preamble three paragraphs to begin talking about the United Methodist denomination, and even then only after it has already defined the church in ecumenical terms and put its finger on "dividedness" as a fundamental hindrance to that church's mission in the world (Discipline, p. 19). Turning to the Constitution proper, Division One, along with our three basic articles about Name, Articles of Religion and Title to Properties (Articles. 2, 3, 6) there are three more articles--all on ecumenism! (Articles. 1, 4, 5 on Church Union, Inclusiveness and Ecumenical Relations).

And when you ask our Articles of Religion and Confession of Faith how United Methodists understand this church, they answer with deep ecumenical insight: as "the one, holy, apostolic and catholic...community of all true believers under the Lordship of Christ," gathered around the Word of God purely preached and the sacraments duly administered. (Articles. XIII, Confession. V). And lest there remain any doubt about what "pure" preaching and "due administration" of sacraments imply, we can be reminded by that basic Constitutional article about "Inclusiveness of the Church" that all persons without regard to race, color, national origin, or economic condition are eligible to attend, participate and share membership in the life and koinonia of this worshiping and witnessing "congregation."

We need to repeat and nail down right from the beginning this fundamental, thoroughly characteristic United Methodism emphasis about ecumenism. "Church unity" has to do not simply with denominational divisions, but with whatever divides and alienates either Christian fellowship or human community: dogmatism and institutionalism, to be sure, but racism, classism, and sexism no less. The emphasis is on "inclusive" church unity. Indeed, the deeper emphasis is upon a church unity whose mission is to bear witness to and visibly demonstrate God's way of healing the broken human community. The key phrase is "inclusive church unity," and the first and basic Division of our Constitution is utterly preoccupied with laying down this foundational United Methodist concept. Do not misread what follows, then, as pleading merely for a narrow interdenominational view of ecumenism; its aim is to make clear this crucial United Methodist concern: ecumenism is missionary through and through.

What is the basis of this fascination with ecumenism as wholeness in church and community? And the answer has to be that it lies deep in the Wesleyan vision of sanctification as the wholeness of salvation; a personal wholeness which is inseparable from a vision of wholeness in church and society. God's gift is the vision and the power for a renewal of this wholeness--a renewal which God freely offers in all and to all without exception. And we are committed to receiving this gift as God gives it, in its wholeness both personally and corporately, and to bearing witness to all, whatever their condition, concerning that gift's "pure, unbounded" powers of reconciliation, liberation and healing. There is a personal being made "perfect in love"; there is also a corporate perfection as God, in the inspired phrase of Charles Wesley, "perfects us in one" *(The United Methodist Hymnal, no. 627)*.

Church unity and church inclusiveness are not mere extras any more than sanctification is a mere extra in personal salvation. They are basic and essential, and in both senses: as unity and as inclusiveness. Wesley, as Albert Outler loved to say, was an "evangelical catholic." One of the most basic meanings of the ancient term "catholicity" is precisely that inclusiveness of the church about which our Constitution speaks. "Catholic Spirit" is Wesley's translation into corporate terms of our characteristic emphasis upon wholeness in personal salvation. There, at the very core of our Wesleyan conviction, lies the reason for our United Methodist ecumenical commitment. We are concerned about church unity because we believe the sanctification of the church belongs to and prepares it for its mission.

That invocation of the traditional Wesley can turn our attention to a fascinating feature of our new disciplinary doctrinal statement *(Discipline* Part II). That statement leaves no doubt that our United Methodist doctrinal heritage consists of two parts: "Our common heritage as Christians" and "our distinctive heritage as United Methodists" (pp. 41, 44). (1) "Our common heritage" as United Methodists is the faith of the apostles and therefore of the scriptural canon, as it has been generally summarized in the ecumenical creeds (the Apostles, the Nicaean, the Chalcedonian Definition) and interpreted in the developing tradition of the great Eastern and Western teachers (Athanasius and the Cappadocians, Augustine and Aquinas, the Continental and the English reformers) all as passed on to us via that unresting editorial pencil of John Wesley in our Articles of Religion.

(2) "Our distinctive heritage as United Methodists" consists of the distinctive Wesleyan sermon themes capable of being preached to coal miners at five in the morning: prevenient grace and repentance, justification and assurance, sanctification and perfection, faith and good works, mission and service, and the nature and mission of the church.

What interests us here is how our church understands their relation. And the answer of our *Discipline* is quite explicit and emphatic: "The core of Wesleyan doctrine that informed our past rightly belongs to our common heritage as Christians" (p. 50). "The heart of our task is to reclaim and renew the distinctive United Methodist doctrinal heritage, which rightly belongs to our common heritage as Christians, for the life and mission of the church today" (p. 56).

Something momentous is being said here about how to relate the common and the distinctive, something that few other churches have said so explicitly as yet. We are stewards of a distinctive tradition on behalf of the whole church, charged to renew and cherish it and to give it to the other churches as something which belongs to their and our common heritage. Our "distinctive" Wesleyan themes are truly ours only within that ecumenical commitment and stewardship. No "distinctives," no United Methodists: that's a truism. But: no ecumenical commitment, no United Methodists either, and that's the point! We can truly have Wesley only by giving him to others in terms which they as well as we can understand. We can truly observe United Methodist services of Holy Communion only as celebrations of the whole church. We can truly have United Methodist ministers and bishops only as recognizable ministers and bishops of the whole church. We can be truly distinctive only as we are one.

Let me try to formulate that commitment into three ecumenical principles: First, The basic United Methodist commitment to the wholeness of God's grace is at once both personal, ecclesial and social. The three unities--personal, churchly and social--are inseparable.

Second: Inclusive church unity is thus constitutive for United Methodism--as constitutive as personal sanctification is for Wesleyan salvation. United Methodism has its being, its integrity, only in relation to the whole church of Christ. We cannot be ourselves without being ecumenical. That is what Wesley saw in his construal of the relation of the Methodists to the Church of England. And it remains utterly clear in principle in the Constitution and Discipline of our denomination.

Third: United Methodism's distinctive heritage is constitutive of and insofar as it expresses the apostolic faith belongs by prior right to the whole church. Our "distinctives" are truly ours only in trust, insofar as we hold them as stewards actively engaged in making them understandable and sharing them with others. This does not deny our mission to the unchurched. But it does take seriously what Wesley knew very well and presupposed in his mission to them: that it is a mission to spread the faith of the one, holy, catholic and apostolic church, or it is nothing. And that requires dialogue with other churches as well as mission to the unchurched.

In a word, ecumenism is of the essence of United Methodism. There can be no more searching question to put to our church than this: What is the health of your ecumenical commitment?

United Methodism's Basic Ecumenical Policy

Can we turn now to policy--those middle points of strategy which link basic principles and quadrennial programs?

I do not have space here for a methodologically explicit derivation of policy from principle. I frankly ask you to follow my attempt simply to focus upon four basic points which belong to any adequate United Methodist ecumenical strategy today.

1. First, deceptively self-evident, yet most basic, is this: The central goal of United Methodism's ecumenical policy is the quest for an inclusive church unity. The reason, as we have sought to make clear, is that church unity is central for our denominational identity and ecclesiology as such.

This church unity focus in our ecumenism is contested by some. Church unity is a North Atlantic concern, it is said; it belongs to the past. The contemporary challenge lies in the broken human community itself, and our concern is not unity but purposeful conflict and surgical use of power. The commanding theme today is not unity among the churches but justice in the human community. Some, then, call for a quite explicit new "secular ecumenism."

If this is posed as an alternative center, I believe that it is a mistake. Gustavo Gutierrez himself insists that the root problem in oppression is not simply unjust social structures but sin, and that any truly radical liberation will begin by generating a new human being. John Wesley agrees: first God's grace, then human response. Thus, no real sanctification without regeneration, and no real regeneration without justification by faith, and no true faith without prevenient grace.

We can translate that into ecclesiological and ecumenical terms. Before the renewal of mission there must be a new koinonia, and before the new koinonia there must be grace and receptive participation in the means by which that grace is "normally given," as Wesley puts it: through the apostolic witness in the scriptures, through faithful contemporary proclamation of that witness today, through initiation into the apostolic community of faith and participation in its communion and mission. The central theme in a United Methodist ecumenical policy, then, must be the quest for church unity as an ecclesial sanctification which is firmly rooted in a new and disciplined openness to the fullness of the "ordinary" means of grace and is therefore capable of bearing witness in its inclusiveness to the healing and wholeness and justice of the human community as well. To make the quest for social justice itself the center of our ecumenical policy is to practice an ecumenism without foundations and to offer a witness without a gospel.

This church unity focus by no means counsels a retreat into ecumenism as interdenominationalism. It asks, rather, that we discern the Body of Christ, as Paul asks, in our so-called ethical issues. Racism, sexism, classism are for United Methodists ecclesiological and ecumenical issues before they are ethical issues. They have to do with how we are the Christian koinonia. That is what our constitutional linkage of church unity and inclusiveness is trying to tell us.

Only a quest for church unity, so understood, will have a message of hope for our post-Christendom contemporaries and a real future in the twenty-first century.

And so our first policy point is: the central principle of our ecumenical policy is the quest for a visible and inclusive church unity.

2. But what kind of concrete and visible sign of this church unity should our policy seek? The question is important, for if church unity is in any sense our task and not purely and simply a divine gift, then it must be attainable, and if attainable then visibly embodied in signs which communicate it. My conviction is that the attainable sign of an adequate United Methodist ecumenical policy must be: visible fellowship in Holy Communion which is inclusive not only of United Methodists but of all persons, especially of those whose liberation is at issue and of those who are members and ministers of other divided churches.

Other concrete signs could be mentioned: various arrangements for common witness, schemes for organizational merger, specific declarations of mutual recognition of other church's baptisms or ordinations, covenanting together with other churches to "live our way toward unity," or conciliar arrangements of various kinds. Section II of our *Discipline* makes it clear, however, that "sharing in Holy Communion with all God's people" is what these many ways point to (p. 88). It is their acid test. "Visible eucharistic fellowship" is not the ultimate ecumenical goal. God's kingdom is the richer goal, but it, too, generates "signs" of its presence, according to the gospels, and this attainable sign of communion belongs to it, and Jesus himself asks us to offer it "in remembrance" of him.

Moreover, this sign is attainable. As it has been threatened and mutilated in history, so it can also be recovered in history.

Is divided Holy Communion that important? Failing to discern the Body of Christ as we eat is that important, according to Paul (I Cor. 11:29), and it is a dangerous symptom in us. I communicate sometimes in a joint "ecumenical" Catholic-Protestant service. We prepare together, repent together, pray together, hear the Word together--and then at the climax of the service turn our backs on each other as we go to our respective Catholic and Protestant ends of the sanctuary to have communion with our God (with our "gods"?). This is behavior I won't tolerate for a minute in a restaurant, yet it is the actual situation every day in every service of Holy Communion, including those of the United Methodists. It is wrong for churches to tolerate that symbol. It points to a sickness in the church. It is right for our Constitution to name that "dividedness...a hindrance to (our) mission" (*Discipline*, p. 19).

The fact that United Methodists are generally ready to accept all others doesn't solve the problem. The solution is not that all become United Methodists, nor all Roman Catholics. The solution has to be sought together. Listening to why others cannot accept our invitation belongs to it. There is plenty of room for all to repent.

And so our second policy point is: the attainable sign to which our policy is committed is an inclusive visible fellowship in Holy Communion as a witness that the Christian gospel can indeed heal broken human community.

3. That point leads to another element in policy: *the unavoidable immediate step toward that goal is to work toward a full inclusive mutual recognition of members and ministers of the divided churches.* We do not need total doctrinal consensus. We do not need massive new structures. Concretely, what we need is mutual recognition of baptisms and ordinations. In other words, we need that mutual understanding of each other which enables an authentic ecumenical hospitality at the table of Holy Communion. And the way to that unity is not uniformity but genuine mutual recognition in each other of the apostolic faith and fellowship--in that good diversity and pluriformity which belong to its contemporary expression.

Three short remarks about that: First, United Methodists have been generous when asked officially to recognize the baptisms and ordinations of other churches and to seek visible eucharistic fellowship with them, as, for example, in the Consultation on Church Union (COCU). The question is: if that generosity is right, are we actively pursuing and broadening it, or are we simply going along when others take the initiative? Where do we stand, for example, with our bilateral recommendation of 1984 "to take steps to declare and establish full fellowship of Word and sacrament" with the Lutherans? Is our ecumenical policy strong enough to generate not simply cooperation and compliance but initiative?

A second remark: It is realized on all sides that the truly tough sticking point in mutual recognition is bishops. And here United Methodists have a problem. It's not simply that John Wesley couldn't recognize our General Superintendents as bishops. Neither can the majority of Christians (e.g., the two-thirds who are Orthodox or Roman Catholics, among others). The answer here does not lie in some unilateral Methodist commission attempting to theologize about our episcopacy. The answer has to lie where our UMC response to the World Council's *Baptism, Eucharist and Ministry* (BEM) text puts it: in our participation in a succession of multilateral projects of reconciliation of ministries, for starters in COCU. I can foresee no widespread mutual recognition of ministers, hence no widespread visible fellowship in Holy Communion, which does not involve, as BEM and COCU recommend, a threefold order of ministry including some version of the historic episcopate as "sign though not a guarantee"--as BEM puts it--of the apostolic (i.e., biblical) tradition as the basis of all ministry, lay and ordained. For that is the issue represented by the ecumenical discussion about our UMC bishops: namely, the question about the "apostolicity," or in our language the biblical integrity, of witness in the United Methodist Church.

This recognizability of our bishops is, when you get right down to it, very nearly the nub of our ecumenical problem concerning an inclusive and visible church unity. And the strategic point is certainly the question now being asked of the UMC by the Consultation on Church Union. Are we preparing our 1992 decision about COCU with sufficient prudence, care, and energy? Our response should be influential to many besides ourselves. We have a responsibility for leadership.

A third remark: Mutual recognition of ministers must include ordained women. The United Methodist insistence on an inclusive church unity has vaulted the UMC way out front in its insistence upon the ordination of women. Mutual recognition of ministers as necessary for visible fellowship in Holy Communion will have to come to terms with this insistence upon inclusiveness.

Briefly, some words of admonition here from one who profoundly believes that this United Methodist "distinctive" belongs to the whole church: (1) This question will not be quickly solved. Not in a quadrennium. Not in a decade. Not, possibly, in a century. Real love is patient, and it was John Wesley who defined ecumenical or "catholic" spirit as real love. (2) It won't help to assume that the right position is clearly known, and that it is our own position, and that the appropriate action for Orthodox and Catholics is repentance. However right we may be in seeing "non-theological factors" here, the discussion is theological, and our case needs to be put in theological terms. (3) To prevail, or even to be taken seriously, those theological arguments will have to show that ordination of women is an expression of the apostolic faith. It is hopeless to concede the apostolic tradition to those who oppose. (4) Likewise, it is insufficient to think that we are talking about merely securing recognition of women as ordained ministers of the United Methodist Church. Our basic ecumenical principles commit us to more. Just as there is no true denominational doctrine except as expression of the apostolic faith; just as there is no denominational bishop except as bishop of the whole church; so there is no such thing as a denominational minister except as a minister of the one, holy, catholic, and apostolic church--the church which our own Constitution puts first. We cannot require that other churches ordain women, though we may work for that. But we must ask for recognition of ordained women as ministers of the only church there is.

And so our third policy point is: the unavoidable immediate step towards the ecumenical goal is to work toward a full inclusive mutual recognition of members and ministers of the divided churches.

4. That brings us to a fourth element of policy. Granted that our ecumenical councils (WCC, NCCC) do not require full mutual recognition of ministers and members or of churches as a requirement for membership, and are thus "pre-conciliar" in character in the technical sense of the term, what would be the basic policy of the UMC with respect to genuine conciliarity? My answer is: the historical embodiment of our attainable goal is best viewed as a future truly ecumenical conciliar event.

We can remind ourselves of the function of an ecumenical council in the classical sense (e.g., in the Jerusalem "council" of Acts 15, or in the Council of Nicaea): namely, as an event called to confess the apostolic faith to the church's contemporaries, a truly ecumenical council means an event in which authorized representatives of all churches come together, when necessary, to exercise the church's universal or ecumenical magisterium (authoritative teaching office). There is no lack of church attempts to confess the faith today. The tragedy is that the church has lost its capacity to speak with one voice. There is no ecumenical magisterium today, and that is a major change from the days in which both Orthodox and Catholic rationales for a universal magisterium were developed. There is no instrumentality for addressing the common Word of Christian faith and hope to our contemporaries today in the name of the whole Christian community on issues of enormous import: abortion, birth control, racism, poverty, euthanasia, nuclear energy and weapons, not to mention such church issues as baptism and "mixed marriages." And though authoritative church teaching today must be rightly and creatively diversified, diversity cannot and should not rationalize the sheer contradiction in church teaching today. And those contradictory teachings are no small reason for what we call the authority crisis today. It cripples witness. Our resolutions end up in archives and footnotes. No particular church can speak for all, not even if its Pope addresses the United Nations. And no present group of churches can either. The WCC constitution, for its part, makes it utterly clear that the WCC has no authority to speak for its member churches any further than they may ask it to do so. "Who speaks for the church?"

And yet the impression grows that the churches are increasingly wanting ecumenical organizations to speak and act on their behalf, especially on issues of high and puzzling technical complexity. Is there a growing conciliar magisterium in our time, and what should United Methodist policy be toward that?

BEM provides a highly interesting example of this problem, and perhaps a hint of the way ahead. Strictly speaking, the WCC is a house in which the churches can carry on an ecumenical conversation with each other. But the churches asked the WCC to do more: to summarize their sixty-year-long conversation on baptism, eucharist and ministry, and to submit the result to the churches.

You know the outcome: unprecedented interest; the Lima text on *Baptism, Eucharist, and Ministry* as the most widely translated, published and used text in modern ecumenical history; six volumes of official responses from the churches published already with a seventh in preparation; a hundred-page WCC analysis of the responses now in the press; plans for a Fifth World Conference on Faith and Order in 1993 to help the churches assess the import of all this for their future relations with one another.

But the most interesting aspect is that the WCC, rather naturally and without much premeditation, did not simply summarize the discussion. It went on to ask the churches four basic questions about the convergence text and its possible role for the churches' lives and ecumenical policy. One church refused to respond, and its letter showed that it understood the point I am trying to make: the WCC has no constitutional authority to ask such questions of a member church, it said. But the astonishing thing is that 189 churches (so far) did not raise that question, but did respond, and moreover wished the project well--including the whole spectrum: the Vatican and the Ecumenical Patriarchate, the Salvation Army and the Quakers, the Pentecostals, and all the major member churches in the WCC.

Moreover, they understood their task to be to respond to BEM from "the highest appropriate levels of authority," officially. The WCC insists that it is not an ecumenical magisterium. But as any teacher knows, questions teach. The WCC has been accorded in these official responses something like a de facto authority as a questioner in the ecumenical conversation among the churches. It is not a mere facilitator or host in the ecumenical conversation house. Moreover, that de facto authority is further attested by the fascinating fact that a number of churches have found it advisable or even necessary to create their own more adequate magisterial instrument in order to produce a response on a level this fundamental.

Our own UMC is an example. As we all know, the General Conference is our highest doctrinal authority under our standards of doctrine. Our General Conference nevertheless saw fit to devise a special magisterial process in order to produce our official response to BEM. Our own ecumenical commission was given authority (and it carried out the task extremely well!) to create a many-sided process of consultation, of local study, of special commissions, of drafting and redrafting, and it was then asked to submit the provisional draft to our Council of Bishops, who, upon realizing the magnitude of the assignment, docketed it in two of their semiannual meetings before they were ready to approve it--unanimously, if I remember correctly--as the official United Methodist response to BEM from our "highest appropriate level of authority."

Curious! The General Conference itself asked the bishops, who have by Constitution no voice or vote in the General Conference where our denominational magisterium is located, to participate in, indeed to consummate, the process of formulating our church's most authoritative response on questions of basic authoritative church teaching. I submit that something more than an episcopacy or general superintendency was stirring in the instincts which created that process.

But our concern here is what occasioned this remarkable constitutional improvisation on our part if not the presence of an ecumenical questioner who we felt in our bones asked questions of us with real authority to do so, and required authoritative answers from us of corresponding weight.

55

What is happening here exceeds our vision, as yet, but it is going to require a United Methodist policy on conciliarity--or, in our own lingo, an ecumenical policy about "connection" and "conferencing." Somewhere between 1990 and a future truly ecumenical conciliar event (say around 2050) will lie hard ecumenical work on developing the presuppositions which can surmount the difficulties preventing such an event today. To name only three: It will have to focus the task of such a conciliar event upon an act of common witness: e.g., on expressing the common apostolic faith and hope to our contemporaries about survival on this planet, and to do so in convergent terms not yet within our grasp. Moreover, such an event would require that we be able to lay our concern before God in a common act of eucharistic worship, a fellowship in Holy Communion still beyond us. Again, such an event would require mutual recognition of all bishops as ministers of the churches' unity in the apostolic faith, and at the same time bring into the event the inclusive representation of both laity and clergy, both male and female, old and young, which our Constitution is so concerned about--an understanding of representation which neither we nor the Christian yet possesses.

I think you see my point. A future truly ecumenical event will have to presuppose some solution to many of our present-day dilemmas. That focusing power is one thing that makes this vision so interesting. And the sharp point of such a vision's demand for United Methodists will be our need for a policy about conciliarity and the ecumenical magisterium. That truly ecumenical conciliar event will happen only if the churches really want it. Does the United Methodist Church want such an event of ecumenical witness?

I believe that we should be leaders in asking for it, as a visible embodiment of a basic ecumenical policy rooted in our understanding of the gospel itself. Like John Wesley, our church understands its own life to require participation in the wider ecumenical church. It believes in the sanctification of the church as well as in the sanctification of persons. It has a missional passion therefore to press for the growth of the ecumenical movement and the common, undivided, unhindered mission of the whole church. It believes that the sign of an inclusive visible fellowship in Holy Communion is not only realistic but attainable in the history of our time (cf. the UMC response to BEM in *Churches Respond to BEM*, Vol. II [Geneva: WCC, 1986], p. 177). And it believes that this process of church renewal is of decisive importance for the healing and renewal of our broken human community today.

And so our fourth policy point is: the historical embodiment of our attainable policy goal is best viewed as a future truly ecumenical conciliar event.

Conclusion

I have tried to show that this ecumenical commitment, these ecumenical principles, and much if not most of these ecumenical policies are already implicit in United Methodism's understanding of its own essential constitution.

My hope is for a basic ecumenical policy in our church which lets the implicit become very explicit--as explicit as the works of love which evidence real faith--as God "perfects us in one."

CULTIVATING THE PASSION FOR UNITY:

Four Key Issues in the Globalization of Theological Education

MICHAEL KINNAMON

There is, I think, a real advantage to having a non-Methodist who teaches at a non-United Methodist seminary help define ecumenical issues for a United Methodist audience. I am free to say, "These are the problems as I see them" without embarrassing anyone in particular. And you are free to say, "Yes, we have those problems, too" or "Thank God we're better off than the Disciples."

I read the survey prepared by Russell Richey and Jean Miller Schmidt* with great interest and appreciation; it caused me to ask how Lexington Theological Seminary would have been able to respond to the questions. We are a school a bit smaller than St. Paul in Kansas City. Our catalog lists thirteen courses that are specifically ecumenical or global in character (though just what that means is a question to which I will return). We sponsor various lectureships and less formal convocations dealing with global and ecumenical themes (the first week in April is designated "Global Awareness Week" with several representatives from the Disciples' Division of Overseas Ministries on campus). Six of our faculty are directly involved in such things as the National Council of Churches' Commission on Faith and Order, the executive committee of the Consultation on Church Union, the board of the Disciples' Council on Christian Unity, and the General Commission on Christian Unity and Interreligious Concerns. We encourage cross-cultural study and hope, within two years, to make it required for M.Div. students. Our student body and faculty are not as culturally or racially/ethnically inclusive as we would like; but we have made progress during the past decade, including the regular presence of visiting international professors. And we are part of an interesting consortium of schools--the Theological Education Association of Mid-America (TEAM-A)--that

*See Appendix 2, pp. 143-150.

includes Asbury Theological Seminary, Southern Baptist Theological Seminary, Louisville Presbyterian Theological Seminary, and St. Meinrad School of Theology (Roman Catholic). Perhaps seventy-five students from these seminaries take advantage of the opportunity to register for a course at one of the other four institutions during our common three-week January term.

Yet even as I offer this list, I feel the need to add two large qualifications. First, these courses and activities do not yet constitute an integrated focus or identity for our Seminary as a whole. Second, I must admit that many, if not most, of our graduates are not particularly passionate about the unity of the church or the renewal of the global human community--and that, of course, is the bottom line.

Perhaps my introductory concerns will gain clarity if I recount a recent experience of our consortium. I proposed last year to the other TEAM-A deans that we approve a course, to be organized simultaneously on each of the five campuses, that would involve our students in direct dialogue encounters.

Well, the deans agreed, but three of them soon reported that they had no faculty members who were able or willing to tackle such a course. The one exception was Southern Baptist. Undaunted, I proposed to teach a "TEAM-A East" dialogue course for Lexington and Asbury students while Dr. William Leonard taught a "TEAM-A West" for Southern Baptist, Louisville Presbyterian, and St. Meinrad students. Again the deans agreed, but when the dust had cleared from registration, we had no one from Asbury or Louisville Presbyterian, three students from St. Meinrad, seven students from Lexington, and twenty-five from Southern Baptist.

I asked a group of Southern Baptist students "why they were so enthusiastic about the course." "Because," they replied, "these issues and our inability to dialogue are tearing us apart, especially each year at convention time." For these Southern Baptists, a willingness to approach theology ecumenically (though they may not quite know what that means) is a mark of their identity. Being ecumenical means something, something rather costly. I also had a revealing conversation with a TEAM-A student representative from Louisville Presbyterian. "Why didn't any students from your school sign up for this course?" I asked. "Perhaps," she answered, "it's because we are ecumenical about everything so there isn't any need."

I hope this brief vignette has already stimulated reflection about the problems and possibilities which bring us to this topic. I want now to become more specific by naming four of the overarching issues as I see them.

Defining the Terms

The first issue is one of definition. What exactly do we mean when we speak of an ecumenical perspective in theological education? I won't rehash the history of the word *oikoumene* and its translations, but I do want to note that the term, in modern usage, has generally referred (1) to the unity and renewal of the whole Christian community (i.e., to the growing relationship among the now separated churches and their common effort to be the one, holy, catholic, and apostolic church), (2) to the world-wide mission of the church (i.e., to the work of the church throughout the *oikoumene*), and (3) to the unity of all humankind (indeed, of all creation), a unity which obviously relates to and finally includes the church.

It is no secret that in the work of the ecumenical movement, the search for visible unity of the church has, at times, been played off against witness or service or social transformation. But I am convinced that this movement, at its best, has articulated a vision of the church and the gospel which powerfully integrates these various definitions and priorities.

We see the foundations of this vision expressed in the 1978 statement, "Christian Unity: Imperatives and New Commitments," by the United Methodist Council of Bishops. "God," the statement begins, "created one world. . .Jesus called into being one church," a church which "was to be the foretaste of the age where the middle wall of partition between nations, races, sexes, and classes--all forms of enmity--had been destroyed." The church, in other words, is not simply the product of a human urge for fellowship; it is, theologically speaking, a gift of God. Our unity as Christians, across all four artificial walls of partition, is not an option on which we get to vote; it is a given which we must seek to obey as part of our participation in God's mission.

I like the way Peter Hodgson of the Vanderbilt Divinity School puts it:

> The exigency for unity does not reside in scriptural proofs (though there are plenty of these) or even in appeals to the classic 'mark' of unity, but in the fundamental logic of Christian faith, which is oriented to a single, central figure and event (God's redemptive action in Christ) and which is intrinsically non-provincial in character (legitimizing no divisions or exclusions on the basis of race, sex, creed, nationality, locale, or language).[1]

Our concern that theological education become more ecumenical in perspective is not an accommodation to the new experience of pluralism or to the realities of the global village (though it clearly takes these into account). It is a response to the gospel of God's universal love and to the definition of the church as one, global, inclusive community of faith.

I need to mention one other dimension of this ecumenical vision as I understand it. The United Methodist policy statement "On the Ecumenical Road" surely understates the point when it says

> We see in none of the existing churches. . .the perfect exemplar of the fullness of the Christian community we seek. What is needed, therefore, is for the now-divided churches to abandon their erstwhile claims to self-sufficiency.

They must also rediscover the spiritual treasures which God has granted to their neighbors who see the gospel from other confessional and cultural perspectives. *The ecumenical vision, in other words, regards unity as essential to the integrity of the faith.* It celebrates our pluralistic context as an enrichment of our attempts to understand and obey the will of God; but it is still God's will we are attempting to understand and obey. As Jane Smith put it, ecumenical Christians hold truth gently. The ecumenical vision, to say it another way, is not philosophically but methodologically pluralistic. An active faith that is truer to the gospel is the goal; expanding the community which seeks, through committed dialogue among differences, to understand the gospel is one crucial means to that end.

I have spent some time on my understanding of the term 'ecumenical' and the vision of the church it implies because it seems to me that this definition is being replaced in many quarters by the notion of ecumenism as interchurch relations. "On the Ecumenical Road" warns of the temptation to settle for cooperation rather than to press for genuine unity through transformation, but I fear the warning has gone unheeded. Our churches and seminaries generally refrain from past polemics and narrowly confessional perspectives, but we often do so, as I see it, in the name of tolerance rather than mutual growth in Christ. The ecumenical status quo is valued for its own sake ("the blessings of diversity and openness") rather than as a constant journey toward deeper, truer koinonia. Our expectations for real unity are so low, and we have become so satisfied with the gains of recent decades, that (unlike my Southern Baptist students) we no longer experience pain of our divisions, the pain of giving such partial witness to the gospel. As a result, there is little passion for ecumenism. When tolerance becomes an end in itself, then cooperation becomes a sufficient goal. But if the very integrity of the faith is at stake, then nothing less than the unity of Christ's Body will suffice.

Actually the situation may be even more dangerous than that. I am now convinced that an ecumenism which is not aimed at transformation of our common life in Christ fosters a relativism which does violence to the integrity of the faith. Our TEAM-A consortium, for example, is characterized by a kind of tolerant cooperation which reinforces present patterns without dialogically challenging our various pet assumptions. Parker Palmer labels this correctly when he speaks of a weak doctrine of pluralism. "Because this notion concedes diversity without calling us into dialogue," he writes, "it leaves us in isolation and destroys community as effectively as the objectivism it seeks to resist."[2]

I hope I have named this issue with sufficient clarity for us to address it. George Lindbeck argues in a recently published essay that theology has for the most part become procedurally more ecumenical, but thematically less so.[3] The question I am posing is whether or not that characterizes the current ecumenical posture in our seminaries. It is clear that we value and embrace diversity, including cultural diversity, as never before. But do we know how to bring that diversity into a dialogue that prompts growth in faithfulness? Are we communicating a vision of the wholeness of the gospel and the church to which students can respond with passion and imagination in their ministries? Have we settled for cooperation and openness rather than the unity of the universal church as a sign and instrument of the unity of humankind?

Ecumenical Amnesia

The first issue, then, has to do with what it means in general to be seminaries marked by an ecumenical perspective. The second issue I want to name has to do more specifically with the teaching of ecumenism in the classroom. Part of the issue is identified in the following statement from the Lutheran ecumenist, Daniel Martensen, in his introduction to the report of a Bossey Consultation in *The Teaching of Ecumenics*. "Visser't Hooft would often say," writes Martensen, "that one of the major failures of the modern ecumenical movement was its inability to perpetuate the ecumenical memory." He was undoubtedly correct. In no segment of the world's Christian population, including faculty and many professional ecumenical staff people, can one assume knowledge of the modern ecumenical movement. From this fact, we can draw an important conclusion about the teaching of ecumenics, namely: unless ecumenics is taught in a self-conscious fashion, it will not be taught at all. It is not enough, he argues, to promote cross-registration among seminaries or to encourage a kind of general ecumenical ethos. Unless the quest for Christian unity and common witness and service is addressed in a concerted fashion and in self-consciously defined courses of study, the ecumenical memory, to say nothing of the ecumenical vision of the future, will be lost.[4]

It is obvious that our schools are far beyond teaching theology or church history or pastoral care or biblical studies from a narrowly denominational standpoint (whatever that might mean). Since Vatican II, we seldom even speak of Protestant theology and Roman Catholic theology as if these were separate streams. And attempts are also being made to avoid teaching from a narrowly cultural standpoint. I suspect that the reading lists for many of our courses include materials written by persons from other parts of the world. But none of this necessarily means that we are teaching students about the growth of the ecumenical movement, that we are fostering commitment to the oneness of the church, or that we are introducing our students to the nature and results of corporate ecumenical dialogue.

I was recently at a meeting of local church educators from the Christian Church (Disciples of Christ) and the United Church of Christ, many of whom were seminary trained. No one with whom I spoke was aware that the World Council of Christian Education, whose roots are in the Sunday School conventions of the nineteenth century, merged with the World Council of Churches in the early 1970s and that, since that time, one of the WCC's three main program units has been entirely devoted to education and congregational renewal. The otherwise excellent and comprehensive text edited by Seymour and Miller, *Contemporary Approaches to Christian Education,* contains no reference to the World Council or other ecumenical bodies. The same can be said, I suspect, of other fields of study as well.

I need quickly to add that being ecumenical should not be reduced to support for a movement, and the movement itself should not be equated with the World Council of Churches. But as Joseph Hough and John Cobb observe, "the WCC thinks globally because its members are from all over the world... [thus] one valuable way of introducing ministerial students to the global context is to make them aware of the work of the WCC in such a way that, as they become church leaders, they will relate the church at all levels to the ongoing world discussions."[5]

Should ecumenics be taught as a distinct area of the curriculum? If not, how do we avoid the tendency to make the ecumenical impulse so diffuse that it is nowhere intentionally fostered? If so, how do we avoid the opposite tendency (seen frequently in the church) to treat ecumenism as a peripheral elective, tangential to the core of the curriculum?

I want to add three quick and somewhat random observations drawn from my own experience. First, I agree with Charles West of Princeton when he writes that ecumenics is an ongoing event--the process itself is the real subject matter; the encounter between living traditions and involved Christians struggling and working with one another. It is important for students to study the history of this process in order that they themselves may become a part of it. But the object of teaching ecumenics is to involve them as participants.[6] The Vatican's "Directory Concerning Ecumenical Matters" makes much the same point: "the first thing to be attended to in ecumenical education is conversion of the heart"--that humility of spirit that makes a mutually vulnerable pursuit of truth possible.[7] That is obviously the premise behind our course on dialogue which, despite its institutional setbacks, is one of the finest experiences I have had in teaching.

Second, I find that ecumenically produced materials are best used hot off the press. There are many problems with theology by consensus and committee, including a frequent lack of depth, which means that such materials do not stand up well over time. For example, the *Sheffield Report* from the WCC's *On Community of Women and Men in the Church* study will not make a good textbook for the 1990s, especially when compared with more systematic treatments of women and the church produced by individual authors. The report is invaluable, however, as a record of global conversations at a particular moment in the church's life and, as such, deserves much more attention than it has received in this country.

Third, I think it is particularly important to acquaint students with ecumenical initiatives currently under consideration in their denominations in order that they can help interpret this work in their congregations. At Lexington, for example, we have devoted two or three public lectures and convocations, over the past two years, to The Consultation on Church Union (COCU) and its plan of covenant communion. The COCU documents are taught in various courses. In the fall of 1991, we hosted a major conference aimed at assessing the response to the COCU proposal in the churches.

Understanding Otherness

The third issue I want to name is raised by the following statement from the president of Union Theological Seminary, Donald Shriver: "Let us grant no M. Div. or doctoral degrees without requiring the candidates to demonstrate knowledge and empathy for a culture, a constituency, a language, a profession, or a point of view decidedly at variance with all that the candidates know most readily. It may be another religion, another country, another ethnic American group, but let us require of ourselves that we will sit in the shoes of this collective, significant other . . ."[8] I suspect that all of us endorse the importance of such an encounter with otherness. We fail the church if a seminary education does not help students resist the temptations of cultural, theological, political, or geographical provincialism. But the question before us is what best enables such stretching of horizons to occur.

The fall 1989 issue of *Theological Education* contains an essay by Robert Schreiter of the Catholic Theological Union in Chicago which argues that intercultural contact usually begins by homogenizing the other, colonizing the other, demonizing the other, romanticizing the other, or pluralizing the other.[9] I hope we will enable students to move beyond these postures to authentic dialogue and empathy--in the classroom, through programs of study and work in other cultures, in the way we worship, through the lively presence of human diversity in our seminary communities.

Tension between the Mandates

Finally, there is a tension in the present life of the church between the two parts of the mandate of the General Commission on Christian Unity and Interreligious Concerns, a tension which at least needs to be named. The Commission's mandate is 1) to advocate and work toward the full reception of the gift of Christian unity in every aspect of the church's life and to foster approaches to ministry and mission which more fully reflect the oneness of Christ's church in the human community, and 2) to advocate and work for the establishment and strengthening of relationships with other living faith communities, to foster dialogue with persons of other faiths, cultures, and ideologies, and to work toward the unity of humankind.

I suspect that most of us can and do affirm both Christian unity and interreligious dialogue as priorities for the church; indeed, we likely see them as complimentary aspects of a common vision rooted in our confession of the universal Creator. But there are obviously many members of the United Methodist Church, not to mention the Disciples and other parts of the one church of Jesus Christ, who reject the theological assumptions behind interfaith dialogue. It is possible to argue that strengthening relationships or engaging in dialogue with other faith communities does not presuppose any judgment of their place in God's plan of salvation, but this is hardly a satisfactory response. If dialogue is defined as a mutually vulnerable pursuit of truth (a definition consonant with the WCC's *Guidelines on Dialogue)*, then Christians presumably can learn something new about the nature and purpose of God from such encounters. The clear implication is that God is at work redemptively in and through these other communities (whose members we regard more as partners in God's work of shalom than as objects of conversion), and that is utterly unacceptable to many in our churches.

My point in raising this is to insist that we hold the tension and to invite us to reflect together on the implications of holding this tension for theological education. There seems to be an increasing tendency for "interfaith dialoguers" and "Jesus only-ists" to dismiss one another as outside the circle of conversation. For example, the well-known historian of religions, Wilfred Cantwell Smith, asserted at a recent meeting sponsored by the WCC that the failure of Christians to affirm the saving action of God not just within other religious traditions but through them is "blasphemy"[10]--a kind of exclusive inclusivism.

I much prefer the position taken by Harvey Cox in a 1988 article in *The Christian Century.* "It is easier for me," writes Cox, "to converse with universally-minded Buddhists or Hindus than with fellow Christians who not only dismiss such people as pagans, but also want to dismiss me for not dismissing them as such."[11] Still, I believe the critically important conversation among people of diverse faiths could founder and fail if we--the dialoguers--lose touch with our fellow believers who cluster on the particularist side. They remind us that without the radical particularity of the original revelation, we would have no faith to share. We remind them that without the universal dream, they falsify the message and diminish the scope of the original vision.

From time to time, we have prospective students at Lexington Theological Seminary who apparently assume that our self-designation as an "ecumenical seminary" means that we subscribe to some new orthodoxy of the left wing, instead of to a methodology that seeks truth in a community of genuine theological diversity. Let me stress that we offer various courses on other faiths, especially Judaism, and are firmly committed as a faculty to the Commission's second mandate (Inter-religious dialogue). But our concern for the first mandate (Christian unity) leads us to affirm that even those Christians who oppose Inter-religious dialogue--or the whole ecumenical enterprise, for that matter --may do so on the basis of principled convictions which, in my opinion, need to be given voice in our conversations.

If I am not out on a limb already, I will end by inching out on one. I speak as a person who loves the United Methodist Church when I say that the biggest objection I hear from your--our--ecumenical partners is that the Methodists are too self-sufficient. When I was in Indiana, we always got strong verbal commitments to ecumenism from the two conferences of the United Methodist Church, but few United Methodists ever showed up at council of churches workshops because these workshops conflicted with "our" Methodist educational events. That story could probably be retold across the country.

My plea, therefore, is that you do not simply ask, "How can we become more ecumenical through our own devices?" but "How can we work within the wider context of schools, programs, and churches to prepare ministers marked by an ecumenical perspective?" Before asking what programs you can develop, ask what existing ecumenical programs you can plug into and support. Before asking what models you can develop for preparing future ecumenical leaders, explore models being developed by ecumenical partners. That in itself would be a significant witness.

Notes

1. Peter C. Hodgson, *Revisioning the Church: Ecclesial Freedom in the New Paradigm* (Fortress Press, 1988), 90.

2. Parker Palmer, *To Know as We Are Known* (Harper and Row, 1983), 66.

3. George Lindbeck, "Ecumenical Theology" in David F. Ford, ed., *The Modern Theologians, vol. II* (Blackwell, 1989), 255.

4. Samuel Amirthan and Cyris H. S. Moon, eds., *The Teaching of Ecumenics* (WCC, 1987), xi-xii.

5. Joseph C. Hough, Jr., and John B. Cobb, Jr., *Christian Identity and Theological Education* (Scholars Press, 1985), 103-04.

6. *The Teaching of Ecumenics*, 93.

7. Thomas F. Stransky and John B. Sheerin, eds., *Doing the Truth in Clarity* (Paulist Press, 1982), 63.

8. Quoted in Edwina Hunter, "Re-visioning the Preaching Curriculum," *Theological Education* (Autumn 1989): 74.

9. Robert J. Schreiter, "Teaching Theology from an Intercultural Perspective," *Theological Education* (Autumn 1989): 19.

10. The quotation is from an account of the meeting by S. Mark Heim, "Mission and Dialogue: 50 Years After Tambaram," *The Christian Century* (April 6, 1988): 342.

11. Harvey Cox, "Many Mansions or One Way? The Crisis in Interfaith Dialogue," *The Christian Century* (August 17-24, 1988): 735.

THE TERMINOLOGY OF ECUMENISM AND INTERRELIGIOUS DIALOGUE IN THEOLOGICAL EDUCATION

JANE I. SMITH

Nearly ten years ago, the Association of Theological Schools in the United States and Canada began to chart an essentially new direction for theological education in North America, one in which the heart of both the faculty and the student body in our theological schools was to be challenged.

To begin this venture, a committee on "internationalization of theological education" was set up, of which I was a member. We soon questioned whether or not "internationalization" was an acceptable term to describe our task. For some of the members, that word evoked the mindset with which we are now so uncomfortable--i.e., Western imperialism. In order to get on with business, we settled somewhat reluctantly on "globalization" as a serviceable description of what we would like to encourage as a major agenda item for our theological schools.

As our discussions continued we repeatedly found ourselves caught in the snares of language. Sometimes a term that appeared to be neutral opened up old wounds. At other times the participants themselves, representing a range of institutions and theological perspectives, used the same terminology but understood it in very different ways. Some of the terms and concepts that emerged in these early discussions are these: international, ecumenical, missiological, inclusive, universal, evangelical, dialogical. When the now popular phrase "globalization of theological education" is used, it is too easy to assume that everyone means the same thing by it. These words and their connotations suggest some of the deep problems that theological educators encounter in the struggle to recognize the relation of the particular to the universal, the church to the world.

The original Committee on Globalization, chaired by Donald Shriver, gave way to the Task Force on Globalization, which continues to meet regularly as part of the committee structure of the ATS. In addition to sponsoring this task force, the Association has been responsible for a range of surveys, reports and publications in the general area of globalization of theological education. Its publication *Theological Education* has been a major forum for articles and exchanges on this topic. A review of some of these essays, published in this journal from 1985-90, will outline the major issues and perspectives on the subject of globalization.

Definitions

In the spring 1986 issue of *Theological Education*, David Schuller, associate director of the ATS and coordinator of the globalization efforts of that organization, provided a summary of the problems that institutions encounter, based on data gleaned in a survey of some one hundred member institutions.[1] These problems can be clustered in several areas: (a) the difficulties of expecting overseas students to be able to function in light of Western cultural particularities and curriculum expectations, (b) the problems of separating Western "good intentions" from disguised imperialism, (c) issues for students, including financial support, language difficulties, and basic living problems, and (d) staffing and financial implications for institutions. Equally important in his identification of these problem areas was his distinction between evangelical concerns and cultural enlightenment .

In the same issue, Don Shriver outlined the major tasks in the project of globalization of theological education.[2] Three of these areas of "ecumenical engagement" are particularly significant for theological schools planning for the 1990s and beyond. These issues are stated in the form of questions for debate: "Should the unity of the church or the unity of humanity be the focus for our understanding of the ecumenical reality?...Is there an inherent tension, even contradiction, between the evangelistic mission of the church and the loving respect owed by Christians to all the cultures, communities and religions of the human world?...Is 'proclamation' compatible with 'dialogue'?" Under the category of "the study of other world religions and Christian mission" (note the combination), Shriver questions whether "it" should be an option or a requirement. In my own years of engagement with interfaith conversation, it has seemed to me that the desire to link the two as Shriver does is somewhat of a false hope. For many, the study of other world religions is precisely *not* for purposes of Christian mission, especially as that task traditionally has been understood.

Understanding versus Proclamation

The discussions of the ATS Committee on Globalization demonstrated that the word *globalization* could serve a range of purposes. Coming at that time from Harvard Divinity School, I brought to the conversation my own concerns: the need to know about Christianity in other world contexts and to know about world religions as a basis for conversation, dialogue, and potential theological growth. Others, coming from different institutional backgrounds, saw globalization as a way to learn more about other peoples of the world in order to bring them the gospel more effectively. When African Cardinal Francis Arinze gave his plenary address at the 1986 ATS biennial, he warned that the careless pursuit of globalization in theological education could result in theological eclecticism.[3] Stressing the importance of being grounded in one's own faith community, Arinze described the theologian as a witness, not as an independent theoretician. He then defined the issue clearly with the following words:

By interreligious dialogue the Church puts itself as an instrument into the hands of divine providence....In such a dialogue the Church discovers the working of God in the other religions...ways of truth which illumine all mankind, and preparation for the Gospel.... (p. 25)

While Arinze stressed the need for balance between dialogue and witness, his concern was that mission be clearly represented in conversation with adherents of other religions:

It would be a mistaken theology to argue that interreligious dialogue should replace missionary evangelization of the followers of other religions....Dialogue and proclamation are both necessary. Christians have no right to deprive other believers of the riches of the mystery of Christ.... (p. 26)

One of the clearest critiques of this position was set forth by Barbara Brown Zigmund, who questioned the distinction between dialogue and proclamation.[4] Dialogue, she noted, is the rational openness to the value of the faiths of other persons, while Christian proclamation stems from "a passionate Christocentric relationship between a person and God." A person of faith would not, or should not, find these two endeavors separable, much less mutually exclusive. Two years later in her own presidential address to the ATS,[5] Zigmund pointed to a growing tension between evangelism and toleration in theological education. Our seminaries see their task as education for three generally separable purposes: conversion, understanding, and appreciation. Witnessing, or evan-

71

gelization, in interfaith dialogue is based on our common humanity as God's creatures. Tolerance in interfaith dialogue is based on the natural differences in the ways God has related to the world. The value of interfaith dialogue in seminaries has to do with appreciating the ways in which we are different rather than in understanding other religions in light of God's revelation in Christ alone, or in pressing for conversion. Her summary comments on that occasion were both accurate and prophetic: "As the ATS pursues its 'globalization' agenda the tension between evangelism and tolerance will continue to haunt us" (p. 48).

At the ATS biennial meeting in which Cardinal Arinze spoke, Don Browning made a presentation entitled "Globalization and the Task of Theological Education in North America" that is considered to be a foundational piece.[6] Browning attached four distinct meanings to the word globalization: (1) the universal mission of the church to evangelize the world; (2) ecumenical cooperation among the various branches of the Christian church itself; (3) dialogue between Christianity and other religions of the world; and (4) the mission of the church to help the poor and disadvantaged of the world. A practical theologian himself, Browning questioned whether theological education can develop educational and theological methodologies that enable students to see the analogies between Christian experience and other kinds of experience. The point is the ability to interpret allegedly non-Christian experiences which our increasingly pluralistic culture provides so that they will deepen a practical global ministry. Browning's reflection that it would take a revolution to train theological thinkers and leaders of the church to share a vital interest in global issues with their congregation is sobering. I believe that this is the task of the seminary today.

The Challenge of Inclusivity

The Association of Theological Schools has also been concerned with stretching the boundaries of theological education to include non-Western, non-American persons. This, of course, is what is meant by those concepts that are already getting frayed by overreference (though probably not by overimplementation) in most of our seminaries: inclusiveness, diversity, and racial/ethnic and class differentiation. In 1987 Gayraud Wilmore stressed that our divinity schools can no longer afford to ignore the demographic changes that are a reality across our country.[7] "The American metropolitan society of this century," he said, "has been impregnated with a cultural vitality and creativity that may be indispensable for the solidarity and renewal of the human community in our time." He identified diversity as not only the presence of non-Christian communities, but as denominational, ecclesial, theological, liturgical, ethical, and spiritual. Complicating all this, he said, is the necessity of a contextual analysis that takes into account other cultural, sociological, economic, and political diversities. I would add that the ATS Task Force on Globalization and its parallel Committee on Underrepresented Constituencies have come to realize that globalization and inclusiveness may not always be compatible.

Another important contribution to the general discussion about globalization, and especially its theological implications, was provided by Robert Shreiter in his excellent article in 1989 entitled, "Teaching Theology from an Intercultural Perspective."[8] Shreiter pointed to the potential distinction between the terms *global* and *inclusive* suggested above when he said that Christianity is challenged both by its own manifestations in other cultures and by the different voices present in American culture. He went on to discuss what he called a third or specifically theological dimension: "In our embrace of a genuine pluralism (where difference is taken seriously), what happens to the unity and normativity of Christian faith?" (p. 15). Shreiter noted that a pluralism that refuses to evaluate is not pluralism at all, but really a kind of indifference or even solipsism and thereby an excuse to abandon the struggle for truth. Christianity has too long been caught in a "sender" rather than a "receiver" mode, he observed, and should now move to combine these in an approach that is more dialogical. Carrying Barbara Zigmund's point to what may be its logical conclusion, he proposed that the only way to accept the other as truly other is to admit that it is possible for the self, in fact, to change.

In responding to Shreiter, Fumitaka Matsuoka raised two questions that all theological educators need to ask before being swept even more rapidly along on the tide of globalization enthusiasm: "What do we really want to accomplish from the multicultural inclusiveness in teaching theology?" and "What are our basic assumptions for teaching and learning theology from an intercultural perspective?"[9] Taking a slightly different tack from Shreiter, Matsuoka suggested that rather than focusing too sharply on differences, it is both appropriate and necessary to seek shared relatedness. In such an encounter, he says, "both parties become conscious not only of their own cultural and linguistic worlds but also of the liminal world that is born between them through encounter with each other's self-concern" (p. 39).

The articles that have been cited from *Theological Education* are only a few of those that have appeared in the past decade on the general subject of globalization. In addition the ATS has sponsored several workshops, the papers for which at present are still in manuscript form.

Two of those, presented in Toronto in 1989, deserve special mention. Fumitaka Matsuoka dealt particularly with the issue of pluralism in the American context.[10] After pointing to some very practical problems for theological education, such as the fact that the cost is often prohibitive for minority and foreign students, he mentioned what many of us have found to be a very troubling reality: the growing gap between theological schools and American culture when the former is making efforts at globalism and inclusiveness while the latter is showing increasing evidence of provincialism, self-preoccupation and racial tension. We are caught, he reflected, in the bind of elitist academic standards on the one hand and denominational provincialism on the other. Matsuoka added that a plural theological conversation must be free to discover what is new and free to revise the agenda in order to move beyond the initial boundaries of inquiry. I will take the liberty of citing Matsuoka's words in this context because I find them so very relevant to our task:

Globalization challenges us to make a shift in our fundamental perceptions and values toward those who are different and "other" from us....Promises without honest experiences and the acknowledgement of pain and alienation offer merely cheap grace. What is needed is more than a mere "exposure trip/immersion" in a foreign setting. One needs to internalize the deep pain of human alienation, of which cross-cultural and cross-gender relationships are a part. Globalization, therefore, does not fit into any developmental model of education because it is disjunctive. It needs to be understood as transformative....

The second of the unpublished papers prepared for the ATS is by Carolyn Sharp.[11] Sharp pointed to something that many of us involved in the study of other world religions have long known. Our potential partners in dialogue may not be at all eager to listen to us, given the history of Christian intolerance. They may, in fact, feel a deep hostility toward Christianity for having to endure the discrepancy between actual Christian behavior and the *a priori* Christian position that Christian faith is liberative and that Christianity is a way of peace. She remarked that we must be ready to deal honestly with the criticism and anger that prospective dialogue partners may bring to the conversations. (In my years of involvement in Christian-Muslim dialogue I can attest to the validity of that observation.) If the cause of dialogue is genuinely to be furthered, she noted, schools of theology must avoid the kind of theological teaching that assumes others would be better off if they knew and accepted the message of the gospel.

Four Major Concerns for Theological Educators

A number of observations could be made about the kinds of issues raised by these thinkers. Some like Matsuoka have tried to get to the heart of the matter by questioning why we are making the push toward globalization in the first place. Others have assumed certain points of departure and built on those. I think those of us who are theological educators in the United States and Canada need to take very serious stock of these concerns and think more clearly about the ramifications of our commitments. As schools and as individuals formulating our ideas in relation both to globalization and inclusiveness, we will not always agree.

(1) Western theoretical and methodological assumptions. Put rather boldly, we need to be very aware of the dangers of educational and theological imperalism. As Sharp reminded us, our colleagues from other national, religious, and racial/ethnic groupings may find it difficult to forget the history of imposition of Western Christian values upon both cultural systems and basic approaches to education.

This concern has several facets. It may mean first that persons from other cultures are quite naturally suspicious of our motivations for wanting to include them, and their perspectives, in our educational programs. It may also mean that when we invite such persons to participate in our institutions, we may be setting them up for a very difficult experience, because we presuppose that their educational training will allow them to succeed in a Western/American context. If they are able to attain admission in our programs at all, they not only must use a language that is not their own but must operate within a framework of educational assumptions with which they may not be familiar.

Our inherent assumptions generally seem to be that such persons will either "learn" to think the way we do and succeed or (unfortunately) give up the venture and go home. This to me is the more subtle and much more dangerous aspect of the matter. We are so throughly grounded in our Western methodological and theological assumptions, and generally so unsophisticated about the viability of other possible approaches, that we can be quite oblivious to our own educational environment. This not only sets up the visitor for the alternatives of changing or failing; it makes it doubly difficult for us to hear and thus profit from the dialogue with these persons.

(2) Globalization as a means of evangelization/dialogue. As I have just suggested, this is an issue of great complexity. Can Western theological educators agree on a common starting point as we analyze

75

our deepest motivations for expanding the arena of theological conversation? My experience suggests that we cannot. Let us say that there is a continuum with evangelism (or mission, proclamation) located at one end and dialogue (or open-ended engagement) at the other. Donald Shriver asked whether the goal of globalization is the unity of the church or the unity of humanity. While he did not relate this question to the matter of evangelization and/or dialogue, that seems to be the basic concern. When it really comes down to it, are we concerned to engage those of other cultures, faiths, and world views in conversation primarily because we wish to share with them the good news of the gospel (in the perhaps unspoken but always ready hope that they will accept this news into their own lives), or are we primarily eager to be challenged by the possibility that our own lives will be changed and our own theological imaginations stretched?

Some of those who have struggled with this issue, such as Barbara Brown Zigmund, would say that this is a false dichotomy because proclamation must be a component of dialogue if the dialogue is to be real, and dialogue and witness are part of the same enterprise. Others would argue that ultimately the two must be in tension because to hold something with conviction, to believe it is true, compels one to say that contradictory beliefs held by others are simply false.[12] Those who acknowledge that tension may find open dialogue incompatible with proclamation (or evangelism ultimately may be incompatible with tolerance). For them, proclamation either presses for conversion or settles for a neutral exchange of views.

One response to these issues has been to say that God is in fact working through all other religions, which provides the common base from which we move to more explicit conversations. Others argue that even this is a very subtle Christian orientation and raise the question of how we can be open to other perspectives without simply presuming that, although appearing in foreign dress, they are in some way consistent with Christian preconceptions. They would cite Cardinal Arinze's notion of "preparation for the gospel" as a kind of presumptuousness.

(3) *Goals and purposes of dialogue.* Related to the issue of whether dialogue and proclamation are ultimately part of the same enterprise is the question: What are the legitimate goals of dialogue? Why do we want to do it and why do we want to adapt theological education so that dialogue can take place? I have been involved in interfaith dialogue conversations through such agencies as the World and National Councils of Churches for many years and have participated in numerous discussions about goals and purposes. A great deal of rhetoric can be boiled down to three distinct reasons for conversation, all of which are

suggested in one way or another by the commentators cited above and all of which need to be considered seriously as we think about the real implications of globalization:

(a) Exchange of information. We want to learn more about each other directly so as to be better, and more accurately, informed. (Participants often beg the question of why such information is desirable or point to the reality of the shrinking world, etc.)

(b) Ecumenical cooperation. The more we know about each other, the easier it will be for us to work cooperatively toward solving issues of poverty, oppression, and global crisis. Here the conversation is moved from the theological to the ethical/practical level, and proclamation takes a back seat to a sharing of matters of urgent and immediate concern. Browning's identification of the role of ecumenical cooperation in helping the poor and oppressed is relevant here. These conversations seem to be essential as we try to solve the problems of how to live together in a world whose very survival is predicated on finding better ways of mutual interaction. It is what one theologian has called the arena for the dialogue of life with life.[13]

(c) Mutual growth. Here we return to some of the questions raised in the discussion of mission and proclamation. It is in the identification of this as a goal of dialogue that participants in discussions in which I have shared have found the greatest difficulty in coming to common agreement. It is here, however, that I believe schools of theology in the West need to make serious, self-conscious decisions if they proceed on the road to inclusiveness and globalization. Do we wish to invite partners to dialogue in order to have our own minds changed? Are we willing to take the risk not only of possibly appropriating the insights of others as part of what we understand to be true but also of accepting the questions of others as our own questions?

When and if the door of possibility for a change of heart and mind is truly opened, the dangers are real. On the one hand, our prospective partners may be duly suspicious of our motivations, as suggested in my first point above. As a Muslim colleague has expressed it, Christians want us to enter the door of dialogue and exit the door of conversion. On the other hand, we may find the very foundation of those things we cherish most deeply shaken in ways that we did not anticipate and do not want. Many a theological student has become involved in study of and conversation with other faith traditions only to find him- or herself uprooted and disconnected from previously sustaining elements of Christian faith.

Shreiter's distinction between a pluralism that refuses to evaluate and one that seriously engages in the struggle for truth is pertinent here.

If in the context of theological education we genuinely wish to engage our students in the struggle for truth, then we must be prepared for the risk. I am convinced that it is only by taking this risk that we are truly engaging in the educative process. Globalization in theological education is ultimately justified because the very process of encounter gives birth to a new world of being together, what Matsuoka has called a "liminal" world. We have the possibility of discovering something new together, neither unrelated to nor unduly constrained by the traditions that inform us and sustain us.

(4) *Globalization vs. inclusiveness.* This concern moves the discussion into a somewhat different dimension. It is clear that by its very definition globalization includes inclusiveness; by opening our institutions to the perspectives of those from other cultural and religious groupings, we force ourselves to be more inclusive. On the other hand, the attention paid to ecumenicity on the global level may set back the progress toward inclusiveness on the local level. According to Wilmore, seminaries must use the wealth of the resources provided by the Christian faith to serve the religious needs of the people in their neighborhood.[14] To do that, we must be sufficiently informed about the needs and expectations of these constituencies. This can present a real conflict with our concern for globalization. Does the inclusion of faculty from Spanish-speaking Latin America really help the needs of our indigenous Chicano communities? Do we simply presume a commonality of concerns among all of the persons who are not part of our dominant Anglo and generally more affluent constituencies? Given the limited financial resources of most of our schools, how do we balance the needs of students from overseas, who often are prevented from working in this country, with financial needs of persons from communities of color in our own neighborhoods? Have we joined the parade rushing toward global inclusiveness and overlooked the needs of those who are closest to us? Have we once again ignored our need to dialogue with and learn from persons in our own country?

Here, then, are just a few of the matters that face us as we consider the benefits of globalization and inclusiveness, and look for new opportunities for dialogue and ecumenical cooperation. We seem to think that "it" is good, although we are uncertain about just what "it" is and are in some obvious disagreement about the nature of the value of its pursuit. We are faced not only with the kinds of theoretical, philosophical and theological concerns mentioned above. We are also caught in the practical bind of limitations in financial and human resources or in the time our students have to spend in theological education. Should we try to do a little of everything or select several things to try to do well, or simply recognize that we have little choice but to continue with a fairly monolithic approach and merely acknowledge to ourselves and our students that there are other possibilities?

Most important, I would argue, is the urgent necessity of serious conversation (inter-institutionally as well as within our respective schools) as to why it is that we wish to create conditions in which ecumenical, interreligious, and cross-cultural exchange can take place. I believe that we must look to the ATS for leadership in helping us to discover which different types of, or goals for, globalization are and are not basically compatible. The implications of this kind of frank discussion are the same for theological education as they are for denominationally and interdenominationally sponsored dialogue sessions. How can we be both "objective" academic institutions and "subjective" participants in ongoing theological traditions?

The boat has already been rocked administratively, pedagogically, and theologically; and choppy waters are ahead whether we like it or not. Seminaries and schools of theology need to decide how, and in what ways, we can provide leadership for the churches in matters of globalization and inclusiveness. (But, as Fredrica Thompsett remarked at an ATS meeting on basic issues in theological education in the summer of 1989, we cannot get so far ahead that the churches are not able to see our taillights.) We were all stirred by the recent speech of Czech poet and president Vaclav Havel to the United States Congress in which he said, "Without a global revolution in the sphere of human consciousness, nothing will change for the better in the sphere of our being as humans, and the catastrophe toward which this world is headed ... will be unavoidable."[15]

I think it is neither trite nor presumptuous to say that those of us involved in the task of theological education do have a major responsibility to assume leadership that many accuse us of having lost. If we can be self-conscious and intentional as we plan for ways in which to meet these challenges, we can be more responsible to our students and more fully engaged partners in a dialogue that promises to be both exciting and essential in the new decade ahead.

Notes

1. David S. Schuller, "Globalization in Theological Education," Summary and Analysis of Summary Data. *Theological Education* (Spring 1986): 19-56.

2. Donald J. Shriver, Jr., "The Globalization of Theological Education: Setting the Task," *Theological Education* (Spring 1986): 7-18.

3. Francis Cardinal Arinze, "Globalization in Theological Education," *Theological Education* (Autumn 1986): 7-31.

4. David A. Hubbard, Henry H. Mitchell, and Barbara Brown Zigmund, "Responses to Keynote Address," *Theological Education* (Autumn 1986): 332-42.

5. Barbara Brown Zigmund, " Theological Education as Advocate," *Theological Education* (Autumn 1986): 44-48.

6. Don S. Browning, "Globalization and the Task of Theological Education in North America," *Theological Education* (Autumn 1986): 43-59.

7. Gayraud S. Wilmore, " Theological Education in a World of Religious and Other Diversities," *Theological Education* (Supplement 1987): 142-64.

8. Robert J. Schreiter, "Teaching Theology from an Intercultural Perspective," *Theological Education* (Autumn 1989): 13-34.

9. Fumitaka Matsuoka, "A Reflection on 'Teaching Theology from an Intercultural Perspective,'" *Theological Education* (Autumn 1989): 35-42.

10. Matsuoka, "Pluralism at Home: Globalization in North America" (Typescript, 1989).

11. Carolyn Sharp, "Dialogue and the Goal of Globalization" (Typescript, 1989).

12. See, for example, Jeffrey Stout, *Ethics after Babel, (Boston: Beacon Press, 1988): "To hold our beliefs is precisely to accept them as true. It would be inconsistent, not a sign of humility, to say that people who disagree with beliefs we hold true are not themselves holding false beliefs" (24-25).*

13. Willem Bijlefeld, "The Dialogue Discussion since World War II--Changing Christian Perspectives on the World of Islam" (presentation to the Committee on Christian-Muslim Relations of the National Council of Churches (January 1990).

14. Wilmore, "Theological Education in a World of Religious and Other Diversities," 147.

15. As cited in *Time* (March 5, 1990): 15.

THEOLOGICAL EDUCATION IN LIGHT OF THE CONSULTATION ON CHURCH UNION

DIEDRA H. KRIEWALD

Early in 1990, Wesley Theological Seminary joined with Washington Theological Consortium to host a conference on youth ministry. Sponsored by the Lilly Foundation, the conference title was: "Aflame for the Future: Youth and the Evangelization of American Culture." The keynote speaker's address was a sophisticated liberal theological critique of North American culture. Western culture, he said, has interpreted the concept of freedom in terms of freedom from limits and freedom for self-fulfillment. This creates a moral vacuum that can only be overcome, according to the speaker, by a "global moral obligation" and a "catholic vision of unity within the inclusiveness of a multi-cultural reality."

While most of the theological educators in attendance were still nodding affirmatively at this wisdom (which many of us take for granted), the pulpit was taken by an articulate spokesman for a counter-culture evangelical position. His response was neither liberal nor polite. The future of the church did not lie within some glorious polyglot, pluralistic cultural environment. That was only a disguise for the cultural conspiracy, headed by technological interests and encouraged by the mass media, to create uniformity in everything from dress and music to politics and religion. The responder called youth to rally to a new Christian "party," one that would celebrate life against the grim effort to create sameness.

Fifty young persons attended the conference as "reality testers." One declared that he did not understand the vocabulary of the presenters. He didn't know exactly what a "catholic vision of unity within the inclusiveness of a multi-cultural reality" might be, or what was implied by a "Christ against culture" position. Nevertheless, he demanded to know why there were so many superficial differences that divided the members of the consultation into denominations, noting that the

Roman Catholics at the conference had Mass at 7:30 every morning, and the Protestants had Holy Communion at 8:00.

The young delegate's question cut through the acrimonious academic discussion between a liberal and evangelical agenda for the church. During the four-day conference, the youth delegates at this event kept pestering adult delegates about church unity. These young people had a vision of a reconciling gospel, and it was one that they simply would not let go.

Despite their tenacity, however, no adult speaker and no responder presented them with any program for Christian unity. No one taught the young Christians that there is the present historic possibility of a new church framework called the "Church of Christ Uniting," at once fully "catholic, evangelical and reformed." No theologian at this consultation engaged the minds and hearts of either young or old with the current plan for a revolutionary covenanting framework now being dreamed into reality by nine Protestant churches (all represented at the consultation). No seminary professor at this conference even hinted that a historic theological agreement has been reached on the apostolic faith or that this consensus heralds "a new kind of ecclesial reality" engendered by covenantal communion in faith, sacraments, ministry, and mission.

The consultation leadership never adequately addressed the persistent yearnings of the young for church unity but proceeded to commission them to go forth into mission. Even the youngest delegates, however, seem to sense the difficulty of doing mission from a divided house. Their concern, I believe, is well stated in the Constitution of the United Methodist Church: "The Church of Jesus Christ exists in and for the world, and its very dividedness is a hindrance to its mission in the world."

A Theological Agenda
Guided by Denominational Interests

The dynamics at the Lilly vision conference are not unique; in fact, they offer a paradigm of what often occurs in mainline theological education and with denomination leadership at all levels. The designers of the consultation never heeded the questions of unity coming from the young because ecumenical convergencies are not a part of their everyday working life and thought.

Most church leaders operate from a denominational perspective that rarely includes the language or root metaphors of ecumenism. Church unity simply did not occur to these church leaders. They failed, therefore, to mention the new possibilities for unity contained in the Church of Christ Uniting or even to point out the exciting ongoing international youth work of the World Council of Churches.

My impression is that, in spite of a few examples of seminary faculty who use the ecumenical texts, Christian unity is seldom seriously engaged in the classroom or its possibilities preached from local United Methodist pulpits. Most laity are as yet unfamiliar with the work of the Consultation on Church Union and are only vaguely acquainted with its implications.

The Church of Christ Uniting

United Methodists at all levels of church governance need to be informed about the twenty years of hard theological work that has resulted in the doctrinal agreements contained in the COCU Consensus.[1] This historic agreement by the nine parent denominations on what constitutes the core of the apostolic faith has enabled a new vision of church unity. The principle document for the Church of Christ Uniting is "Churches in Covenant Communion: The Church of Christ Uniting."[2]

COCU is a concept of unity in which member churches retain their own denominational names, identity, church governments, liturgy, and patterns of ministerial training and placement. Yet, COCU is a new ecclesial reality in which the partners in covenant will accept an irreducible minimum of eight "elements" which include a common apostolic faith, recognition of members in one baptism, and mutual recognition and reconciliation of the ordained ministry.

This is not a plan to build a new superchurch: COCU rejected a plan for institutional union in 1970. COCU is essentially not a political but a theological structure that will enable the nine members of this Protestant faith to join in visible table and pulpit fellowship. Through the acceptance of mutual ministries, the partner churches intend to build a more effective mission to the world.

The Importance of Immediate Education

Ecumenical education is critical at this moment in the history of the church. The nine participating denominations in COCU are called to take action within five years by the highest governing body of each church. The next General Conference meets in 1992. Five years is not a very long time to convince a large and diverse membership that the new ecclesial reality of a reconciled and reconciling household of faith is a better way than the parochial interests of denominational self-preservation.[3]

A short timetable makes it urgent that seminary educators and denominational leaders immediately become intentional advocates for the Church Uniting. Neither laity nor clergy have yet discovered the implications for our common life that may be transformed by national, regional, and local covenanting councils contained in the consensus.

If we wish to make a difference in this historic moment, there are at least four teaching initiatives that United Methodist seminaries (and conference leaders) could undertake to bridge the knowledge gap between the ecumenical representatives of the denomination and the general constituency of the church.

Four Initiatives

1. Sharing the Best-Kept Secret

The best-kept secret in the United Methodist Church is the theological consensus for covenanting approved by the Sixteenth Plenary of the Consultation on Church Union in 1984. The name given in 1988 to the nine churches seeking covenantal communion, the Church of Christ Uniting, is virtually unknown in the annual conferences. A totally unscientific and informal poll of students at my seminary produced disappointing but not unexpected results. "Is the Church of Christ Uniting the same as the United Church of Christ?" "Is the Church of Christ uniting with another denomination?" Most students had heard the acronym COCU but could not give the initials definition or content. Often I heard the common perception: "COCU? I thought it died earlier in this decade." Only one student knew about the Consensus and could name the partner churches. The Peninsula Conference had sent the documents to all pastors, including student pastors, and this very bright young man had paid careful attention.

The first initiative of the seminaries must be simply informational. Ways must be found to inform faculty, administrators, staff, and students about the Church Uniting. For many in the seminary community the ecclesiastical reality of a Church Uniting will be entirely new data. Some will immediately ask questions about "merger" and will need to read the basic documents for clarification. The eight elements of covenanting found in the document "Churches in Covenant Communion" are particularly important.

If United Methodist seminaries are to become centers of information on the Church Uniting, a good beginning would be to stock bookstores and libraries with the critical texts. Our careless stocking of an ecumenical library is a predictable indication of minimal scholarly interest. In addition, one of the valuable gifts seminary scholars give to the church is in the area of research and writing. Interpretive essays on the Church Uniting written for denominational publications would be welcome. Whether in the classroom, on the lecture circuit in annual conferences, or in research and writing, denominational leaders should enlist the talent in its seminary faculties to help the denomination answer questions of the sufficiency and claim of the two consenting documents.

2. Do "Others" Pass the Test?

Traditionally, questions around church unity involve issues of doctrine or polity. The question then becomes whether the questing partners are on the "orthodox" side of that issue or not. But it is rarely a simple yes or no proposition. In official ecumenical conversations, if the theological water is too acidic, delegates may literally take an Alka Seltzer and come back to the table after dinner. Faced with the same situation, church members who are unfamiliar with the issues may not know whether to return to the table for further discussion.

Litmus tests on membership, doctrine, liturgy, and ministry are a temptation for those just entering the ecumenical process. Since the majority of the membership of the United Methodist Church will soon be joining into this multilateral conversation, partisan interest groups within the body should be encouraged to be restrained in lifting up one narrowly drawn issue or another as a litmus test for unity. Most United Methodists will never be able to enter into the theological struggles that produced the covenanting document. However, the initiative of the seminaries to teach and interpret the basic documents in pastor's schools, retreat settings, and local congregations would go a long way toward facilitating an understanding of the process of covenanting.

If the first task of the seminaries is disseminating correct information about the content of the Consensus and the process of covenanting, then the second initiative to follow is a conscious decision to be interpreters of the documents. The first responsibility, of course, is "in-house" education. How will the COCU documents find their way into the seminary curriculum? The history of the ecumenical movement, for example, is now considered by many scholars to be a teaching discipline with its own set of texts and traditions. Where is this history being taught in seminary courses? How does this current history become as "alive" in our seminary life as the Reformation or the Evangelical revival? Some church historians believe that we are living in a time of ecclesiastical formation as important, in its own way, as the early church councils were in their time.

The learners that we educate in the seminary environment become the teachers of the faith as they return to student pastorates on the weekend. The only information that many congregations will receive on the Church Uniting will come from student pastors. Surely, then, one key to unlocking the interpretive treasures of this emerging vision of the church in its wholeness is in the hands of United Methodist seminaries. The seminary communities can become centers of information and interpretation to help restore balance and discourage litmus testing, which artificially limits the ecumenical dialogue.

3. But Don't We Celebrate Diversity? Then Why the Quest for Unity?

Can't you hear it: "We were just getting used to the celebration of diversity!" Diversity is officially affirmed in United Methodist seminaries. Uniformity is sought, however, by each interest group within the community. Feminists are determined to change exclusive language. African-American seminarians are committed to eliminating racism. Evangelicals fear that relativism and universalism are undermining the particularity of the gospel. Those influenced by liberation theology lobby the rich on behalf of "God's preferential option for the poor." Seminarians whose first language is not English advocate for their own history and culture in the classroom. Each interest group is dedicated to a just cause.

Sometimes, however, partisans openly denigrate Christians who advocate agendas they do not understand or deem worthy. It is not always easy to achieve harmony and neighborly love in a climate of diversity. What, then, is the true nature of diversity in a seminary environment? Is it a rich symbol of the Body of Christ or an uneasy reminder of a fragmented church that is "crippled in proclaiming a reconciling gospel to a broken and divided world"?

The affirmation of diversity in United Methodist seminaries is welcome. But an environment where "differences are affirmed, accepted, and celebrated" desperately needs a point of focus. Cultural relativism, with the proposition that all intellectual positions are equally worthy and all ethical standards are of equal value, has become an attractive option for North Americans, including many seminarians. This view threatens to break down the true foundation of diversity in the seminary.

The commitment of the nine partner denominations to seek visible unity with wholeness through the COCU Consensus is thus very timely. A church truly "catholic, evangelical and reformed" provides order and stability in faith, ministries, sacraments, and mission. The watchword of the Church Uniting is "Unity without Uniformity." The Church Uniting document locates the question of the "diversity, equality, and dignity of all persons" in a powerful "Confession of Faith" (Consensus: V. 17, p. 32). Diversity does not depend on sociological trends or subjective feelings; instead, diversity is affirmed and inexorably linked to thankful confession. The language is even stronger in the latest document.

Is it possible to have unity and differences? Yes, if unity is understood as it is in the COCU consensus as "a gift to be made visible."[4] The time has come to set the justice agenda into an ecumenical framework. Annual conference cabinets might take the initiative to study and live out the model of unity proposed in Consensus II and III. Those seminary faculties that do their intellectual work in theological consortiums are ideally placed to live as ecumenical advocates and to initiate conversations on the Church Uniting with other schools.

5. Is it Wesleyan?

No one knows for sure how our spiritual progenitors would have regarded this plan. Scholars have written persuasively of the distinctly "catholic" nature of the Wesleys' thought. John Wesley utilized Anglican, Moravian, Reformed, Lutheran, and Eastern Orthodox ideas in his theology. We ecumenists suspect that he would be pleased with the Church Uniting and ask Charles to write a new hymn celebrating this time of covenanting. Methodist leaders certainly have made an enormous contribution to the ecumenical conversations through the years.

The nature of teaching authority is of critical importance for all denominations in the climate of relativism that dominates our society. The cultural diversity of the United States impinges on almost all the major decisions we make concerning ministry in our conference structure. The climate of extreme individualism in doctrinal matters fosters a lack of purpose and direction in the church. In response, some United Methodists urged the General Conference of 1988 to implement stronger doctrinal standards from the early Wesleyan tradition. In this present quadrennium, commissions have been mandated to study baptism and same-sex relationships and to continue the process of trying to order our ministries. United Methodism has no clearly designated *magisterium*, or teaching office, to help us decide such matters. We are a conciliar church, and the ultimate decisions in faith and order belong to the General Conference, whose rulings make their way into the *Discipline*.

As the nine denominations come to covenanting, each must face squarely the question of how much authority to accord its own history and traditions. How much weight should United Methodists in the closing years of the twentieth century give, for example, to John Wesley's or Francis Asbury's understanding of faith, sacraments, and ministry? Wesleyan questions are internally useful within the denomination. The authority to become a member of the Church Uniting, however, probably does not rely so much on each partner's traditional ancestors as on the ecumenical convergencies of this century.

Ecumenists would claim that the question, "Is it Wesleyan?" is not the most important query in the long view. The truth is that the major agendas of our denomination as well as the docket for the larger order in the body of Christ is being ordered by a new kind of *magisterium*. The teaching office to which we all attend is located somewhere in the structures of ecumenical dialogues. There is no one location and no one teacher. At one time, a teaching consensus emerges from the Faith and Order Commission of the World Council of Churches. At another time, a teaching consensus emanates from the many bilateral discussions that continue among the denominations.

The best example of the power of this ecumenical teaching office is in the content of the *United Methodist Book of Worship*. To be sure, the final product was a denominational labor of several years. Wesleyan theology has always been shaped by a sung liturgy, and this new hymnbook will form our self-identity for years to come. The amazing new form and feel of the sacramental liturgies, the rite of Christian Marriage, and the service of Death and Resurrection, as well as the new Morning and Evening Prayer services, are instantly recognizable and consistent with the liturgical forms found in equally new Episcopal, Lutheran, Presbyterian, and United Church of Christ hymnal and service books. A consensus on suitable hymnody for our time has grown across denominational lines during the past two decades. The agenda for our worship life in Christ has been transformed by a spiritual power that seems beyond the scope of any one denomination.

In the same way, it is possible that the theological consensus of the COCU covenanting document will also drive the agenda as member denominations consider issues of the ordering of ministries. Inter-denominational commissions, as the one we have currently discussing baptism and confirmation, must carefully take into consideration the conclusions already forged in ecumenical consultations, or our denomination will lose credibility in the world of the universal church.

Make no mistake, however; our traditions and heritage are of vital importance not only to us as United Methodists but also as we contribute our unique vision of the gospel to the larger body of Christ. In the Uniting Church that identity is affirmed and maintained. The fact is, however, that something larger than individual traditions is driving the basic agenda of emerging church doctrine and policy. A case can be made, therefore, that the faith and order of the church is no longer shaped in the academic academy of the seminary, or in the local politics of individual denominations. When the churches began to pray for church unity several decades ago, we were unprepared for the fact that God does answer prayer. A new glimpse of church life is taking its shape in all kinds of interfaith discussions. Seminary faculties will need to play an ever more important role in the balancing act so essential to a Church Uniting; that is, continuing in the task of maintaining a living Wesleyan tradition (discouraging Wesleyan fundamentalism) while participating in and advocating for the current reformation of the church.

Conclusions

Five initiatives await seminary action.

1. Share the secret of covenanting communion by becoming information centers for the Church of Christ Uniting.

2. Commit to interpret the ecumenical documents in a way that will provoke and stimulate but will discourage litmus testing.

3. Accept a formal or informal mandate to help the denomination answer questions of sufficiency and claim.

4. Model unity without uniformity in seminary and consortium life.

5. Encourage a balance between the Wesleyan heritage and the ecumenical convergencies which now consciously or unconsciously drive the agenda of the body of Christ.

Reformation is a living reality in the body of Christ. Prayerfully and quite seriously we may need a converting moment in our denomination --a moment when we consciously choose to become members of a new confessing family of faith. In this moment we purposefully move out of our self-identifiable turf and thrust ourselves into the yet unknown winds of the Holy Spirit.

This essay began with one event in the Lilly Foundation Consultation on Youth ministries. For many youth and young adults the church is on trial. They search for a meaning system and a commitment worthy of their lives. Again and again, persons of all ages ask why there is so much division and denominational self-absorption. The Church of Christ Uniting is a worthy vision for all generations.

Those of us in seminary education have the task of teaching and interpreting that vision. We need to recruit and recruit and recruit new leadership for the ecumenical future. The call for seminary educators to exercise a measure of the teaching office is abundant and clear. There is also the option, of course, that we may be the last to know.

Notes

1. Gerald F. Moede, ed., *The COCU Consensus: In Quest of a Church of Christ Uniting*, (Consultation on Church Union, 1985). Copies are available from the Consultation on Church Union, Research Park, 151 Wall Street, Princeton, N.J., 08540-1514.

2. *Churches in Covenant Communion: The Church of Christ Uniting*, (Consultation on Church Union, 1985). Copies are available from the Consultation on Church Union (see note 1 for address).

3. Excellent study materials on the Church of Christ Uniting are available from the General Commission on Christian Unity and Interreligious Concerns of the United Methodist Church (GCCUIC), Room 1300, 475 Riverside Drive, New York, N.Y. 10115.

4. *Churches in Covenant Communion*, p. 17, pars. 8, 9, 10.

THE UNIVERSAL AND THE PARTICULAR IN MUSLIM–CHRISTIAN DIALOGUE

LAMIN SANNEH

The modern western encounter with Muslims may be characterized by three major trends. Beginning in the early 19th century, Western Christian missionaries were sent to Muslim countries, supported by a sense of optimism about the sheer number of potential Christian converts. The second trend, beginning in the late 19th century, is the study of Islam in Western universities as one branch of what has been called Oriental Studies. At first, this study was motivated by a sense of confidence in the Western ability, as a child of the Enlightenment, to understand Islam with a detached, rational perspective. After the collapse of the European colonial empires, however, Western guilt became a powerful motivating force behind the academic study of Islam. The third major trend is Muslim-Christian dialogue. In the post-World War II period, primarily in Western Europe, dialogue became the main channel for discharging a lingering Western guilt over the abuses of colonialism and for stirring Christian repentance at having denigrated Muslim religious views and practices.

The shift to dialogue, while the most recent, is also the most painful stage in the Western encounter with Muslims. Both Christian mission and Western orientalism were buoyed by a sense of optimism: missionaries and academics anticipated success, whether it was based on premillennialism or on social Darwinism. By contrast, the shift to dialogue coincided with a Western liberal pessimism about the value of religion in general and Christianity in particular. In this perspective, religion amounted to no more than a phase in the ongoing human enterprise. Western theologians, for the most part Protestant, engaged in dialogue in an attempt to transcend religious differences, which were seen as vestiges of a less enlightened mode of being.

Dialogue and Western Secularity

However, the West's attitude was not necessarily shared by the rest of the world. By using dialogue to overcome religion, the West in its liberal phase once again intruded on other people's religious inheritance. How did it accomplish this? Christian liberals, strongly influenced by Western secular philosophical values, had the habit of taking liberties with their own declining church. This hardened them toward other religions, leading them to make faulty assumptions on their behalf. But the irony is this: in discounting the affirmations of Christianity, the liberal West constituted itself into the arbiter of all other religious affirmations. Thus, in spite of its widely celebrated decline, Christianity continued to shape liberal interreligious discourse. This dialogue proceeded to ignore the empirical religious situation in favor of ideological assertions. Western antireligious rationalism constituted itself as the universal paradigm: if non-Christians were consistent they would be convinced of the Western position, and that would validate Western intellectual ascendance; if they were not, it would show the gap in the West's favor.[1]

At its simplest, the secular liberal disavowal of religion erects a wall that obstructs all enlightened efforts toward the goal of global understanding. Religious distinctiveness, and the diversity it fosters, is indispensible to the cause of human solidarity. Allow people their sense of ultimate trust and loyalty and they will most likely reciprocate with gestures of goodwill. It is from the sense of commitment and obligation that dialogue and the other forms of mutual encounter arise, making conversation meaningful rather than superfluous. As the African proverb has it, a one-legged person does not dance. Interreligious dialogue without distinctive claims based on ultimate truth is a lame creature indeed.

In spite of indubitable evidence of a global religious revival, the modern secular West is set on a relentlessly antireligious course, intending to sweep the rest of the world into the wasteland of a religionless world. Abandoning distinctive Christian claims, however, diminishes from the total pool of religious traditions and restricts the scope of diversity. It also puts pressure on others to do likewise, drawing them into a circle of mutual likemindedness. The time may be right to urge a different kind of pluralism in which neither the Muslim nor the Christian should be required to disown his or her particularity as a precondition for dialogue.

A New Model for Mission

In order to turn this one-sidedness, we need to look at the conciliatory work of Kenneth Cragg. In the second edition of his epochmaking book, *The Call of the Minaret,* Cragg invites us to take a fresh view of mission, seeing it not as the insensitive imposition of Western Christianity or Western culture on others but as the crucible for challenging the Western cultural monopoly on Christianity. In this connection, he writes, "The Gospel as such has no native country . . . Christ belongs to us only because he belongs to all."[2]

Cragg suggests that faithfulness in mission constitutes an important safeguard against the "vulgar universalizing" of Western culture. Mission brings us within range of others besides ourselves. As long as we are prepared to communicate to others an "account for the hope that lies in us" (1 Pet. 3:15), we will remain within striking range, so to speak, of new discoveries and fresh possibilities. Mission is--and has always been--Christianity's credibility option. It is not simply that Christians perpetuated Western mistakes in mission (although they did that, and worse) as that the church came to its Pentecostal fulfillment in an unprecedented variety of tongues and cultures. It is not uniformity so much as diversity and particularity that mission promoted.

More than any other single factor, it is the vernacular Scriptures that have held together the vivid array of nationalities and cultures that comprise non-Western Christianity today. The translation of the Bible into indigenous languages has effectively displaced European languages and the cultural traditions they enshrined. Furthermore, it established a momentous source for indigenous self-understanding:[3] not only was it a medium for the transmission of Christianity; it also supplied a means for evaluating Western influences. The local appropriation of the message of missions thus helped to mitigate the disruptive effects of overseas Western commercial and political exploitation. It is, therefore, a legitimate question whether Western missions, in thus providing the means wherewith indigenous societies might defend themselves, did not also profoundly alter the self-image of the Western church.[4]

The common charge that Christian mission was Western cultural imperialism, or that witness was only a cover for Western arrogance and intolerance, needs seriously to be qualified. Cragg contends, on the contrary, that there is no better challenge to Western cultural attitudes than exposure to Muslim claims and affirmations. Furthermore, it is the Christian obligation to Christ that brings the Christian within range of that exposure. And what holds true for the Christian is equally true for the Muslim: without that which distinguishes the Muslim as a

Muslim the call to witness as a Muslim is meaningless, and encounter with others unnecessary.

It is necessary to unpack the many issues Cragg raises by his comparative observations. First, it is clear that no one starts from an absolutely neutral point of view. It is not given to us as human beings to occupy a universally objective position, one that transcends human particularity. Whatever the claims and counterclaims, however we affirm or renounce our tradition or other people's, or whatever our fruit-salad strategy towards religious differences, we are always and inevitably having to do with specific bits and pieces that combine in a given situation for certain individuals and groups.

Therefore, whether we do simple or sophisticated analysis of religious claims, and, even if we postpone thinking about them, we remain rooted in space and time. The ground from which we proceed remains fixed. Consequently, our defense of universal truths as Christians and Muslims brings our own particularities into the service of universal obligation. For Christians the danger is to distill the truth of the incarnation as having only anthropological status, while for Muslims it is to use divine transcendence to discount human initiative. In the Christian case a religious premise would be employed for a this-worldly end, while in the Muslim case it would be employed to deny any humanistic end. Where Christians derive non-religious consequences from religious premises, Muslims make religious doctrine depend on human enforcement, though not human initiative. Christians and Muslims differ in their attitudes towards vernacular cultures, but both imply that culture is a common mediatory channel for religion.

The Value of Particularity

In the past we have held that particularity condemns us to at least two hard, unfruitful choices: one that cripples us with a one-legged view of God's intention, and the other that denies the value or point of dialogue. I believe that these two choices are inadequate for understanding the full potential of particularity since they merely repeat a version of the one-sidedness we identified in Western liberalism.

Let me spell out in more detail the implications of the criticism of particularity. There is first the view that particularity conflicts with human solidarity, that those who advocate it also deny the oneness of the human family, and that particularity promotes sectarianism rather than pluralism. In fact, this is a misunderstanding of particularity that should be distinguished from the ideology of exclusivism, also called *particularism*. Particularity, on the other hand, refers to the specificity and concreteness of the human situation. Human beings are not disembodied, free-floating spirits, unattached to time and place. All that we know, claim, feel, observe, and have is grounded in distinctive and particular ways of being human. There is no such thing as Miss or Mr. Universal Humanity. We all bear particular names, speak particular languages, live in particular places, and have particular tastes (and distastes). The general science of anatomical study, for all its value, can reveal nothing of that rich particularity. The category of *homo sapiens* is at heart a social classification.

Religion fits into that scheme of particularity. In its detailed prescriptions, its general teachings, its rules of liturgy and observance, and the powerful currents of loyalty it stirs in our beings, religion reflects and promotes human diversity and particularity as geometry builds from the void the fluid curves and sharp, detailed angles that give form and shape to particular figures. The Muslim is a Muslim because Islam creates a distinctive identity different from that of the Buddhist, the Hindu, the Jew, the Marxist, the nationalist, and, of course, the Christian. Without the distinction, there can be no identity, and without identity there is no basis for the defense involved in witness, or for dialogue. And without that distinction, too, we run the risk of "the vulgar universalizing" of our particularity about which Cragg warns.

If Christians offer to Muslims a religious discount of Christianity because they want to take Muslims seriously, for example, then they must *either* imply a similar move for Muslims, which would be just a version of Christian unilateralism, or else concede the truth of Muslim claims, which leaves them with conversion as the only viable option. In either case, whether it is Christian unilateralism or conversion to Islam, Christians will only have traded in different versions of one-sidedness rather than advanced the cause of genuine dialogue.

The other possibility, of saying that a Muslim's religion is his or her business, may appear to leave the Muslim safely alone but in fact rejects beforehand Islam's own claim to universal attention. Of course, Islam is the business of the Muslim so far as responsibility for it goes, but it is a responsibility that includes witness and mission. We cannot restrict Islam to Muslims or Christianity to Christians without reducing religion to one-sided mutual indifference.[5] An African proverb says that when a dead leaf falls, its neighbor does not laugh, for the fate that befalls it is reserved for its neighbor, too.

Some people have sought to escape these stark choices by opting for selective pluralism. They pick and choose among various religious teachings and claim the result as containing all that is best and vital in religion. Yet even that piece of bold and generous syncretism scarcely resolves the difficulty. If you take elements from two religions, let us say, and merge them, you create a third which differs from the other two in its particular form and style. But you would have thus incurred the additional hazard of having created by poaching a third religion believed now to be superior to the others, a form of one-sidedness that defeats the whole purpose of pluralism. I believe that this approach is the hidden agenda of much of what passes for comparative religion and the philosophy of religion.

We should not confuse particularism with particularity for the same reasons that we must hold together dialogue and witness in inter-religious encounter. If as a Muslim, for example, you really do not believe that Islam demands conviction in you and others, then dialogue is a tedious diversion, and so, in fact, is the whole edifice of Islam. Yet if you feel that dialogue is important enough to relinquish the distinctiveness of religious claims, then you have made dialogue the new source of overriding claims on you, and dialogue itself judges what is true or false in religion. For example, we might now encourage dialogue because it promotes human solidarity and religious pluralism, believing that those values are greater than any other religious claim, but we would not have escaped the exclusive one-sidedness even of those values. We would thus recall the particularity of religious development and thus would merely have retraced the circle. Or we may have done worse by creating an illusory substitute for religion.

Similar grounds persist with the Christian interest in dialogue: if Christ's claims on us are not valid, then dialogue with Muslims in the name of Christianity is a subterfuge, and that is a hollow foundation for any meaningful conversation. If we claim that there are other urgent reasons why we must engage in dialogue with Muslims, we imply the need for similar urgent reasons for Muslims, if not at the beginning, then hopefully before or at the end of our meeting. Yet the question will not go away: why should we make "our more urgent reasons" grounds for a more secure commitment than the claims of Christ? Why should conviction in mutual trust and tolerance be worth it if, for the Christian, it requires denying that "God was in Christ reconciling the world to himself"? If the name means anything at all, then we have a responsibility for it; and if it does not, then we do not bear it. Thus, religious particularity involves an identity and a responsibility for such identity. Of course, it matters how and by what means that responsibility is discharged, which explains why dialogue and witness constitute an important challenge, being two sides of the same coin. Reticence about who and what we are is not a hopeful sign of human maturity, especially since we fill the silence with unexposed prejudice. "Worse than silences," Cragg admonishes, "are the vetoes" we invoke against each other.[6] Dialogue and witness go together, and they balance and enhance each other. The responsibility for witness incurs that of dialogue, and vice-versa: I can listen because I may also speak, and the other persons know because their listening and my speaking, and viceversa, are intertwined. "They who take Christ are in a state of perpetual discovery. And the discoveries they make are made through the discoveries they enable."[7]

All this is of pointed concern for Muslim-Christian dialogue. The separate claims of Muslims and Christians to the obligation for mission and witness have often led to stalemate and intolerance. The divisive nature of talk about mission and witness appears to justify the tactic of avoiding these tough issues. After all, profound misgiving in the West about this question has created the false combat of liberal humanists and conservative evangelicals: the former reject witness and thus make dialogue pointless, while the latter defend witness but consider dialogue surrender, or even a betrayal. When it comes to Muslim-Christian dialogue, liberals may think it a good thing to suggest to Muslims that they have an adequate conception of Christ, a Christ emptied of much of his orthodox identity; and conservative evangelicals may feel exclusive about their own witness to Christ without coming to grips with Islamic notions of finality. Thus, liberals and conservatives would have merely cooked each other's goose. Somewhere in the middle ground we have to find a way to move beyond religious unilateralism.

Witness and Dialogue: the Critical Frontier

Several sharp questions indicate the nature of the problem we face. If Muslims are obliged to witness about their faith to non-Muslims, does it not mean that non-Muslims may also speak about Islam? Conversely, if Christians wish to convince others of the truth of Christianity, does it not stand to reason that others can give an account of the gospel in a way that indicates their own understanding? In other words, witness implies the capacity for mutual comprehension and with that the basis for accepting the integrity of the other even where disagreements exist. In our very particularities we have reason for respecting each other. Retreat from particularity unravels all the interlacing patterns of human mutuality, stripping it of coherence and comprehension. No abstract formula can be an adequate substitute for human or religious solidarity, especially since such formulas are themselves the extrapolations of one side or the other.

We must press further. If the non-Muslim or the non-Christian can speak *to* and *of* the other side, as obviously occurs in witness and dialogue, then he or she can speak *for* it as well. In other words, dialogue and witness assume a capacity for entering someone else's experience not just to find what is similar but to see the distinctiveness. Particularity thus implies responsibility for our differences. Therefore, Muslims may justly look to Christians for partnership in projects of Islamic witness, and vice versa.[8] Muslim eagerness to witness to the truths of Islam should admit collaboration with Christians as Christians, and viceversa. That implies a similar degree of commitment in Christians to the claims of the gospel and a similar commitment of Muslims to the claims of Islam. It is not simply that Muslims wish to set out the facts about Islam and leave the matter there but that setting out the facts commences the witness for which dialogue exists as counterpart. Ultimately, the response sought is submission to God as Islam frames it. Yet in a pluralistic context, religious propagation has often to be content with less than full conversion, and Muslims and Christians need to recognize the freedom of people actively *not* to be Muslims and Christians. It means, for example, that non-religious persons may speak searchingly enough about religious claims to require serious rethinking by religious people. To that extent even non-religious outsiders may speak to the essential matters of religion. Obviously, there are areas of complexity: a measure of sympathy is required for any deep comprehension, but any religion that promotes itself through commendation invites and justifies the role of external interlocutors. Islam cannot escape this any more than Christianity. And, for what it is worth, are we not ourselves, in terms of any notional universality, "outsiders" to God, although we claim to possess the message?

Thus our respective religious claims bind us to each other, not simply in the fortuitous circumstance that we wish to convert each other (which in any case only God can do) but in the profound sense that our respective distinctiveness is constitutive of our truth-experience. It turns out that what we have in common is our participation in the enterprise of God through the particularity of time, place, and language, so that even our universal claims will evaporate as illusory if we cut the ground from under ourselves or each other. The common challenge in Islam and Christianity to witness is also a challenge to participation, to be involved in "a spiritual transaction as well as a physical adjacency."[9] We need to be aware of the fact that all religious claims are intended for human custody even where they direct us to transcendent ends. As a result, religion schematizes such claims in human terms. Just as we should be careful not to confuse God's terms with our terms, so we must recognize it is our carefulness that is doing duty for God. It is, therefore, impossible to separate witness to God's truth from the human initiative of dialogue. Thus we proclaim the truth as criterion also of dialogue. It is, for that very reason, a hazardous undertaking, for it is easy to play God to others and do so from no more an exalted position than the wish to see our particular cultural forms predominate. If we say that persons must believe in God by first believing our testimony about God, have we not made divine "believability" dependent on human "believability"? And can we do this without taking God's place? That is to say, can we do this without absolutizing the medium of our commendation? I believe, in fact, the claims of Christianity for the Christian and those of Islam for the Muslim should help check the tendency to assume that ours is the only vehicle, a view that can only trample on others.

If we assume that it is valid for outsiders to form an accurate enough impression of our religion to give or withhold their assent, then it follows that what Christians say about Islam and what Muslims say about Christianity matters enormously. We cannot exclude outsider interest in our affairs without disqualifying those affairs from having a claim on others. And religious exclusiveness may reassure a jealous regard, but it will also invite negative dismissal.

Mutual Criticism

In fact, Muslims and Christians have spoken about each other, sometimes with a striking lack of inhibition. Muslim writers, for example, have repeated the traditional strictures against Christianity and diagnosed what they see as Christianity's inherent flaws. They have gone on to deride the religion in its Western setting, alleging ills in Western society that are imputed to the church's failure. In his book, *Social Justice in Islam*, Sayyid Qutb denounced Christianity as inherently "unable except by intrigue to compete with the social and economic systems which are ever developing, because it has no essential philosophy of actual, practical life."[10] Summarizing the burden of the dismissal of Christianity made by modern Muslim writers, Cragg writes that in their eyes

the Christian Church is incurably compromised with hypocrisy and vested interest. The Christian ethic is vague, impractical, otherworldly. It has set impossible standards of moral purity--and every form of corruption, prostitution, and vice has flourished behind its idealist facade. Better the sound, moderate, feasible sanity of Islam, with its recognition of the weaknesses and limits of human nature, than the futile idealism and real shame of Christian society. Christian history, likewise, is a sordid record of compromise and bigotry, broadening out into the proliferating sins and scandals of Western civilization. Christianity is jejune, effete, misguided, and discredited. Its origins are erroneous, its story tarnished, and its energies spent.[11]

The Muslim impatience with Christianity may sometimes lead to a sharp mocking and derisive tone. One modern Muslim author, Khalil Gauba, in his book *Prophet of the Desert* comments on Christ as follows:

Poor Jesus Christ expressed the noblest sentiments on charity and forgiveness; thus upon the Cross, persecuted and crucified, he forgave his enemies--'They know not what they do.' But it was never in Christ's good fortune to have his enemies reduced to impotence before him.[12]

In the sectarian Ahmadiyya Muslim Movement this derision of Christ is carried to extreme limits. According to Ghulam Ahmad, the founder of the Ahmadiyya, the cry of Jesus on the Cross was cowardly and pathetic, even ignominious; and there are even aspersions on his moral character on a scale to rival *The Satanic Verses*. Yet, as Cragg rightly observes, "We must avoid the easy temptation to vindication....Assertions such as this [are] not overcome by [their] like....Here are not arguments to be refuted; here is a tragedy to be redeemed. What matters is not that Muslims have thought ill of Christianity but that they have misread the Christ."[13] In fact, we may say that what matters is that Muslims demonstrate by their criticism the unflattering limits of religious one-sidedness, a reminder that outsiders are tempted to quick judgments, and for that reason should learn in dialogue the value of mutual correction and commendation. Religious particularity is not incitement to aggression but the call to courage under patience. At any rate, if it turns out that even "outsidedness" is no disqualification from criticism, then it becomes clear that retreat is not a viable option, and consequently it is all the more urgent that our judgments be grounded in mutual penetration of each other's testimony and intention, including a patient regard for the hard facts adorned with the soft virtues of faith, devotion, and hallowed memory. For after all, whether we claim universality for ourselves and particularity for others, or viceversa, whether we defer to others or ignore them, we are all marked by the common paradox of human contingency and divine obligation. Consequently, Christian witness, and its Islamic rejoinder, or Muslim witness and its mutual Christian response, cannot retreat into stalemate or recrimination.

In that and other senses Muslims and Christians stand together. (It is a little unfortunate to use the metaphor of standing together, with its combative notion and that of closing ranks against others. It might be truer to speak instead of surrendering together, of a humble submission in the divine presence. But let that pass.) Both Islam and Christianity began and expanded as religions addressed to outsiders. The Qur'an repeatedly calls nonbelievers to ponder its message: to consider, to remember, to reflect, to observe, to bring to mind, to pay attention to, to attend to the signs of God, all that so thinking persons might mend their ways and turn to the Lord. We would have a rather emaciated and an invalid Qur'an were we to expunge from it all the passages addressed to non-Muslims. The book rings with the accent of outsiders and in parts sweeps forward with a rehearsal of objections to itself. *Ma zannukum bi-Rabb al-Alamin?* "What do you suppose of the Lord of the worlds?" (xxxvii: 87) In that question the Qur'an invites its hearers to ponder and reflect on who God is, not the God of abstract logic but the God who fashioned the world and now invites our attention. Rather than assume our answer, the Qur'an formulates the question and leaves the final issue to us. In that sense Islam is the question that demands our answers, although more often than not we think Islam is the answer that removes our questions.[14]

Even when it pronounces on the quality of the response human beings give to its message, the Qur'an may criticize inadequate or misdirected human response but seldom the need or responsibility for the response. In several passages this point is made clear: *Ma qadaru Allaha haqqa qadrihi,*[15] "They did not esteem God as He should be esteemed," or "They did not measure God by God's own true measure." In other words, God's criteria (*haqqa qadrihi*) are far more exacting than ordinary human standards, although clearly we are not thereby excluded from God's standards. The rigorous thinking we must do with reference to the things of God reminds us that retreat is not our choice nor indifference our calling. The Qur'an is loud and clear about the duty of attentiveness lest we incur the offense of "unthinking" heedlessness, *ghaflah*. We can see from all this that had the Qur'an been addressed only to bona fide Muslims then it would have been a very different sort of book.

There is a further step to be taken in the matter of right understanding, and that is clarity about what we are urged to respond to. How do we know unless we are told? And how can we be told unless we can take it in? That immediately suggests that the message bearer has to assume a measure of integrity in the hearer, so that the "outsider" is, as it were, privy to the truth before it is announced! It is for the sake of outsiders that prophets tune their senses and refine their spirits in order to deliver into their hands the word that began with God and in God. And so the prophet Moses, like Isaiah after him, prays, "Loose the knot from my tongue that they may understand what I say."[16]

Religious people, of course, are well practiced at putting themselves in the right, and thus beyond the range of the censure of their own Scriptures. If Muslims have done this, they could not have better company than Christians. Right through the Bible there rages a volcanic controversy between God and the people set up to be God's witnesses. The prophets have priests and kings by their ears and assail them with words we normally reserve for our enemies. Yahweh exhausts himself with swearing at his people and then relenting. Jesus despairs of his disciples, their slowness of mind and hardness of spirit, and in turn rebukes, cajoles, threatens, curses, encourages, assures, and instructs them. Then the apostles pick up the theme with recalcitrant congregations, wild individuals, and strange customs. We do not get in the Christian Scriptures a tidy, uniform, closed inside track of faith and salvation. Thus, both Christianity and Islam would appear to deny that religion reinforces only creedal uniformity.

One way we have dealt with the issue of outsiders is to convince ourselves, in the way we have failed to convince outsiders, that all religions are similar and that, for example, Muslim claims to finality of truth have their counterpart in Christianity, and Christian differences are also mirrored in Islam. In other words, Islam is a reflection of Christianity, and viceversa, so that to understand each other we need only to understand ourselves. All such attempts to "include" Islam in our framework play back to us our own ideas and scales of familiarity and promote in not-so-subtle form the notion that we know the truth about others sometimes even better than they themselves. This view of the matter normatizes our own particular one-sidedness and invites others to do the same for theirs. It sets back any prospects for mutual understanding.

Let me be quite clear. If common ground could bring about the sorely needed rapprochement between Muslims and Christians, then it would be inexcusable not to claim it. In addition, if Muslims could be convinced that Western depictions of their world are accurate and persuasive, then we need go no farther. In other words, if the issue were merely one of offering our assurance of good intentions for a genuinely harmonious pluralism to come about, then clearly toil and labor would be pointless. But it would come at the cost of making Muslims, or Christians, mere duplicates of the other. Even if we were able to achieve such unilateral disposition of our differences, it would be false to one side or the other. But I am afraid we may be deceiving ourselves by ignoring, and thus perpetuating, close to twelve hundred years of recalcitrance, ignorance, and mutual recrimination. Something is terribly wrong with our relationship, so wrong that when our medieval predecessors saw common ground they traded charges and countercharges of stealing and unfaithfulness. In the Crusades Christians went to war against Muslims because the similarities in Islam proved the Prophet stole from Christians. Muslims for their part argued that Islam had superseded a defective Christianity. Common identity was ground for common mistrust. The secular impatience with such religious obduracy is understandable, but the secular remedy of ignoring religion altogether creates space for more assertive forms of religion.

Christian-Muslim Reconcilation

Few scholars have carried on their shoulders as great a burden for the centuries of interreligious mistrust, weighed these matters as judiciously, and explored their historical and spiritual ramifications as sensitively as has Kenneth Cragg, himself the embodiment of Christian-Muslim reconciliation and the symbol of genuine encounter. Part of his confidence rests in his view that reciprocity is possible and needed from the Muslim side. Many reasons can be adduced for this, including that of challenging Christians to come out of isolation and domestic preoccupation. Long before science and technology shrank our world into a close-knit community of economic interests, our religious traditions postulated a universal God who had dominion over all our affairs. If Western science and technology have replaced such a universal God with the fruits of human ingenuity, then it is a serious question whether, given the particularity of the Western scientific enterprise itself, they represent a greater possibility for trust and neighborliness than that represented by our respective religious claims.

It is no idle speculation to say that science and technology, for all their wonderful gifts to us, have also bequeathed a legacy of divisiveness, destruction, mistrust, and exclusiveness little different from religions. Yet religions at least contain the elements of an antidote in the form of self-criticism. In that sense, no religion can be a barracoon and still be genuinely missionary. As Cragg expresses it, "It is only in mission that truth comes to its own crisis--a crisis from which the very thrust of mission can all too easily exempt it. A faith, such as Islam or Christianity, that is denied if not commended cannot be satisfied merely to coexist. Yet only in coexistence can it pursue its commendation."[17] Christians who seek God's will in witness have in effect brought themselves within range of the exacting demands of Jesus' prayer, "not my will, but thine, be done." It is to those higher tasks, deeper scrutinies, and larger sympathies that witness brings the Christian. Nothing searches more than the measure by which God esteems us. And for Christians the particular name of Jesus Christ sums it.

Dialogue, therefore, needs to be seen beyond the squint-eyed focus of Western debunking and one-sidedness and linked to witness if it is to open new horizons. The deference of liberalism in merely adopting Muslim particularity as the test for meaningful dialogue covers very little ground, while the conservative defense of Christian exclusiveness elicits its religious and secular opposite. Consequently, the West seems paralyzed from the left and from the right, two extreme wings that in their opposite tendencies prevent movement.

The Third World Challenge

One hopeful sign of a way forward is the enormous expansion of Christianity in the non-Western world, an expansion that has brought Third World Christians into new responsibility for witness and dialogue. There is, of course, an important qualification with the recruitment of Third World Christians by Western organizations for participation in dialogue meetings. Such participation often involves subscribing to unstated but real Western liberal assumptions and seeking to acquit oneself by the standards of one's benefactors. In spite of such major obstacles, it is nevertheless likely that dialogue for Third World Christians will emerge in the context of genuine religious commitment, not as the unilateral outlet for a residual Western superiority complex. Thus, the emergence of non-Western Christianity in both its Protestant and Catholic forms signals a new development for the church and provides an exciting context for exploring the opportunities and challenges of Christian particularity.

One major difference, for example, is that, unlike Christians in the West, Third World Christians have emerged from a profoundly pluralist religious and cultural world, a fact that deepens their understanding of the gospel, whatever other inadequacies they may have. Whereas Western Christians often make the assumption that religious pluralism occurred after the formulations of Christianity had been put in place, Third World Christians know their Christianity is part and consequence of pluralism, rather than an exception to it. For many of them, responsibility for pluralism is one side of the coin and responsibility for Christian particularity is the other. This largely explains why, when Western Christians are calling for an end to Christian exceptionalism (what some have called the "myth of Christian uniqueness"), Third World Christians for their part are calling for greater application of the gospel in church and society.

Picking up an issue that bears a strong resemblance to the problem of Western unilateralism, the American historian C. Vann Woodward writes that the white world has assumed black history to be nothing more than the effects of white people on black society.[18] The fact that Third World Christians are setting their own agenda implies a shift from preestablished Western categories and is thus hopeful for all concerned, however threatening in the short term it may be to Western hegemonic claims. As the Ecumenical Association of African Theologians stressed in a recent conference, the central question for them is "the mission of the church *today*."[19] Western pessimism, therefore, contrasts with Third World confidence, just as its retreat contrasts with the glad celebration of the other.

Notes

1. In a highly polemical piece, the American scholar and self-avowed apostle of liberal relativism, Arthur Schlesinger, Jr., set forth a grisly catalogue of the wrongs of Christianity and, by implication, of all religions. He wrote: "It is the belief in absolutes . . . that is the great enemy today of the life of the mind . . . history suggests that the damage done to humanity by the relativist is far less than the damage done by the absolutist . . . the great religious ages . . . were notorious not only for acquiescence in poverty, inequality, exploitation and oppression but for enthusiastic justifications of slavery, persecution, abandonment of small children, torture, genocide." Arthur Schlesinger, Jr., "The Opening of the American Mind," *The New York Times Book Review*, July 23, 1989.

2. Kenneth Cragg, 1956, *The Call of the Minaret*, second edition (Maryknoll, New York: 1985), 167-68.

3. Henry Venn (d.1873), the pioneer Secretary of the Church Missionary Society in London, expressed a similar view when he wrote in implicit criticism of British colonial expansion in Africa: "The breath of life in a native Church [was] self-government, self-support, self-extension." Cited in W. Knight, *The Missionary Secretariat of Henry Venn* (London, 1882) 416. Colonialism sought efficiency for its justification while missions sought "active response and co-operation from the people," a divergence of approach stemming from the divergent nature of mission and colonialism. J.F. Ade Ajayi, *Christian Missions in Nigeria, 1841-1891: The Making of a New Elite* (London: Longmans, 1965; reprinted Evanston, Il.: Northwestern University Press, 1969) 174.

4. I have dealt with this issue in my recent book, *Translating the Message: The Missionary Impact on Culture* (Maryknoll, N.Y.: Orbis Books, 1989).

5. Cragg warns of the dangers of a protective vigilance about one's own tradition outside a common obligation to the world and to each other. In that case religion acts as a force for division, insulation, and separation in a world otherwise brought together by the forces of science and technology. Kenneth Cragg, *Alive to God* (London: Oxford University Press, 1970) 8ff. Such protec-

tive vigilance, in fact, merely encourages mutual indifference to which our own religious tradition cannot be immune. "We are not alive to God if we are dead to each other," says Cragg, *Alive to God*, 6.

6. Cragg, *Minaret*, 234. We cannot disqualify theological predicates, which is what Muslims and Christians often wish to do for each other, unless in fact they "describe" one God. In this way our very controversies are about a common faith, but conversely, that common faith is controversial within its unity. Cragg, *Alive to God*, p. 17n.

7. Cragg, *Minaret* 168.

8. A Muslim tract, *Islam Explained*, written by Abdul Jalil of the Al-Huda Islamic Center, Elberton, Ga., lists as one of its distribution outlets the National Council of Churches of Christ of the United States of America. The tract speaks with full confidence of the claims and teachings of Islam, including the idea of Islam as the confirmation and completion of monotheist religion. It would be a major advance if Christian churches are accorded similar freedom and facility in Islamic countries. All sides are challenged to a similar consistency of responsibility and reciprocity lest one side's particularity becomes exclusive of the other's.

9. Cragg, *Minaret*, 204.

10. Cited in Cragg, *Minaret*, 221. For a treatment of the thought of Sayyid Qutb, see Kenneth Cragg, *The Pen and the Faith: Eight Modern Muslim Writers and the Qu'ran* (London: George Allen and Unwin, 1985) 52-71.

11. Cragg, *Minaret*, 222. Kalim Siddiqi of the Muslim Institute in London is equally forthright in his condemnation of the West and the exclusive claim of Muslims to God's truth. He writes, "The position that has to be taken now, and only the Islamic Movement can take it, is that the western civilization is in fact a plague and a pestilence. It is no civilization at all. It is a disease. It feeds upon itself to its own detriment. The west today is qualitatively no different from the *jahiliyyah*, the primitive savagery and ignorance that prevailed in Arabia and the rest of the world at the time of the Prophet Muhammad." Kenneth Cragg, *Jesus and the Muslims: An Exploration* (London: George Allen and Unwin) 284. It is difficult to avoid observing that the openness of Western society to the Muslim presence itself is what enables and protects such views which would be inconceivable for Christians in Muslim countries.

12 Quoted in Cragg, *Minaret*, 227.

13. Cragg, *Minaret*, 222.

14. Writing of Christianity in this regard, Cragg says that "the duty to bring others to Him who asks ['What do men say that I am?'], that they may answer for themselves" remains a Christian responsibility. *Minaret*, 235.

15. vi:91; xxii:74; xxxix:67.

16. Qur'an xx:27-8. See also Cragg, *Minaret*, 275.

17. Cragg, *Minaret*, 201.

18. Woodward writes: "For however sympathetic they may be, white historians with few exceptions are primarily concerned with the moral, social, political, and economic problems of white men and their past. They are prone to present

to the Negro as his [*sic*] history the record of what the white man believed, thought, legislated, did and did not do about [*sic*] the Negro." C. Vann Woodward, The Future of the Past: Historical Writings (New York: Oxford University Press, 1989).

19. This is published in a report, *La Mission de L'Eglise Aujourdhui*, Kinshasa.

THE GLOBAL–CONTEXTUAL MATRIX IN THE SEMINARY CLASSROOM

M. THOMAS THANGARAJ

I would like to preface my reflections on globalization with some autobiographical notes. I have been working as a theological teacher in South India, at the Tamilnadu Theological Seminary, Madurai, from 1971 onward. It was in the early seventies that the call for "contextualization" came powerfully to us in India, especially through the collective wisdom of a series of consultations on theological education held in India during the earlier decades and through the leadership of the Theological Education Fund of the World Council of Churches.[1] Anything from outside our own context --national or regional--was seen as something to be rejected, or at least suspended for the moment. Those of us who were trained in the theologies of the West were asked to put those theologies on the waiting list and immerse ourselves in "Indian Christian Theology." Any talk about the "global" was seen as a threat to, or a betrayal of, the process of contextualization. This call to contextualization looked quite convincing not only because of biblical and theological convictions but also because, under the leadership of Prime Minister Indira Gandhi, there were posters all over India which said, "Be Indian, Buy Indian." Even during the period of my study at Harvard (1980-83), the "local" took precedence over the "global" in my thinking and research.

But now I am teaching courses at Candler in an area called "World Christianity". Under the umbrella of this topic, I am expected to "interpret the experience of and developments in the churches outside the United States to the churches in the United States, historically, theologically, and culturally." Quite a formidable task indeed! The interesting thing is that I am doing just the opposite of what I have been doing in India as a theological teacher. In India, I was enabling my students to engage intensely in the local context, while at Candler I am inviting my students to go beyond their context and look at the global reality, both ecclesial and human. Thus I am involved in the "globalization" of theological education at Candler. Yet in another respect, I am doing exactly the same thing at Candler that I did in India. In both situations I am telling my students that it is not enough if they have read Barth, Tillich, Kaufman, or Cobb; they should also have read M.M. Thomas, C.S. Song, Sankara, Radhakrishnan, and a host of others. Therefore, in my autobiography, these two concerns--globalization and contextualization--have come together. With that as the background, I want to reflect on globalization in theological education in the United States.

Globalization as Contextualization

I am convinced that globalization is the best way, and perhaps the only way, to do contextual theological education in this country. There are two major reasons for this. First of all, it is becoming more and more evident that we are able to recognize the contextual character of our own theological thinking only when we engage with theologies which have arisen in contexts other than our own. As long as we are not exposed to other "contextual" theologies, we fail to detect the contextual character of our own theology. From 1978-81, in the department of systematic theology of the Tamilnadu Theological Seminary, I had a colleague from Sweden. When I visited him in Sweden in 1985, he told me, "Thomas, the one thing that I learned in India was that there was something called Swedish Christian theology!" An exposure to Indian Christian theology had led him to this new awareness. For centuries, theologians in the West had assumed that they were doing a theology which was a theology not controlled or constrained by the demands of their own context. Even Karl Barth, who did work out a thoroughgoing contextual theology for his own day, was quite unwilling to be self-consciously involved in constructing a contextual theology. In the introduction to his *Church Dogmatics*, he wrote:

I believe that it is expected of the Church and its theology--a world within the world no less than chemistry or the theatre--that it should keep precisely to the rhythm of its own relevant concerns, and thus consider well what are the real needs of the day by which its own programme should be directed. I have found by experience that in the last resort the man in the street who is so highly respected by many ecclesiastics and theologians will really take notice of us when we do not worry about what he expects of us but do what we are charged to do.[2]

Therefore, it is important that theologians and theological students are exposed to theologies which are self-consciously contextual so that they will be enabled to recognize the contextual character of their own theologies.

Secondly, in understanding one's own context, it is imperative that one perceives the interconnectedness of that context to other contexts. When this is not recognized, one's perception of the context and the contextual issues becomes either blurred or distorted. For example, the questions of ecology and environment, which are very contextual issues for the United States, can be understood only in a global context and through an international perspective. Similarly, contextual issues concerning Christian ministry are better understood in the light of global realities and problems. Thus, only through a process of globalization does one fulfill the task of contextualization.

To enable this kind of a globalization to happen in our seminaries, the presence of a few visiting professors from countries outside the United States or an increase in the percentage of international students in our schools is not enough. We need to adopt an entirely different theological and educational methodology in all the courses that are taught in our schools. Each subject that is offered in the seminary or school should be taught in such a way that the global-contextual matrix of that particular discipline is highlighted and explicated. In this process of contextualization through globalization, the national faculty of our schools have a much more important role to play than the international faculty.

Globalization as Missionary Mutuality

Another aim of globalization is to develop an understanding of the mission of the church that is rooted in the local and open to the global. The modern missionary movement emphasized overseas missions to such an extent that our vision of the global church got distorted, and we began to see ourselves as "sending" churches and "receiving" churches. A growing number of our students are disillusioned and guilty about the mission of the church. For most of them mission has come to signify domination and subjugation of other cultures, religions, and peoples, rather than the sharing of the message of liberation in mutuality and solidarity.

The international community within our schools is partly responsible for this kind of disillusionment and guilt. By sharing the horror stories of the missionary era, we have successfully raised the consciousness of Christians in the First World with regard to the excesses of the missionary movement. But what we need now is the development of a sense of mutuality and partnership in our missionary vocation. Here again the process of globalization has a significant role to play. The international students and faculty in our schools need to be viewed more as missionaries-in-residence than simply as students and teachers.

To enable the emergence of such a sense of mutuality and partnership, theological schools need to be in partnership with churches and theological schools in other parts of the world, especially the Two-Thirds World. Very often, international students are admitted into our programs and international faculty are appointed as visiting professors without any reference to the needs, demands, and programs of churches and theological schools in those countries. My own perception is that it is better to have mutual and sustained relationships with particular churches and schools abroad than to extend an open invitation to the international community to come and help in the process of globalization. Open invitations often lead to competition and a lack of understanding with regard to the actual needs of the churches in other parts of the world. The task of globalization should happen within the context of a concrete form of partnership so that a new and refreshing form of missionary mutuality may emerge. For example, the D.Th. program of the Senate of Serampore College in India is structured so that every doctoral student spends a year of study abroad in a school that is already in partnership with Serampore College. This is an excellent case of missionary mutuality.

Globalization as an Expression of Solidarity

The process of globalization, as we are aware, is not limited to intra-ecclesial cooperation and mutuality but involves the larger socio-political and religio-cultural global reality. I am sure that most of our schools offer courses on world religions and international politics and economics, and in some of our schools, this area of study is seen as part of the foundational requirement of the curriculum. In addition to reading and understanding world religions and global socio-political issues, I plead for a search for concrete forms and expressions of solidarity with the larger international and interreligious community.

This concern can be addressed in two ways. First, we can be constantly on the lookout for occasions when we can express our solidarity with the larger global community. Most of our seminaries and theological schools are located in cities and towns where there is an international and interreligious community. For example, there are 4,000 Hindu families living in Atlanta and at least three Hindu temples. The process of globalization can be greatly enhanced through the expression of solidarity in their festivals, worship, and community life. In a similar way, we can promote globalization through expressions of solidarity during times of various international events and crises, such as the independence of Namibia, the fall of the Berlin wall, the massacre at Tiananmen Square, the Persian Gulf War, and so on.

Secondly, by enabling our students to spend at least a brief period of their study program in a country other than the United States, we can enable them to express their solidarity with the people of the globe. My own feeling is that our students widen their horizons and understand human solidarity to a far greater degree by spending significant time outside the United States than by merely being exposed to the token presence of international students and teachers at their own school. This became true when I took a group of Candler students on a Travel Seminar to South India last summer. Here again, one needs to work out the dynamics of such a program in full partnership with institutions and churches in other parts of the world. There are times when the churches and theological institutions in the Two-Thirds World see the task of educating the people from the First World as an additional burden to bear, while the education of their own students is understaffed, under-equipped, and often financially strained.

Globalization as Inclusive Pedagogy

Theological schools are primarily institutions of education, not international social service agencies. This means that the task of globalization cannot be seen as an added program or an appendix to the work of the school. The spirit of globalization should permeate the very pedagogy of the school so that the teaching and learning method takes the concerns of globalization into account at every stage. This is a pedagogy of inclusivity. How can we teach the Bible adequately without including the hermeneutics of the liberation theologians from all over the world? Is it possible or desirable at all to teach the history of Christianity without taking into account the stories of women, Afro-Americans, and other oppressed peoples? Questions of this kind should inform and shape the pedagogy of our schools.

When I use the word *inclusivity* there are two possible dangers. First, it is possible to limit the discussion of inclusivity simply to the question of gender and race within our own national or regional context. I am always surprised by the way the word *multicultural* is used in our theological discussions. Very often, I find that it is confined to the inclusion of women and ethnic minorities in this country. We need to develop a larger concept and vision of inclusivity than that. Secondly, while inclusivity can be defined too narrowly, there is also the other danger of defining inclusivity in such a wide and encompassing manner that the local is swallowed up in the global. During the past two years I have met several Afro-American and women theologians who see the whole process of globalization as a cover-up for local injustices. This charge gains credibility because of the fact that it is much easier, and perhaps more exotic, to hire an international faculty than hire a woman or an Afro-American. Globalization can be more a threat than a help!

While noting the dangers, however, we still need to press on to work towards a pedagogy of inclusiveness. One of the prerequisites for such a pedagogy is an educated faculty--a faculty who are exposed to and familiar with the global concerns in their own disciplines. This may mean liberating our faculty from their prison of over-specialization, letting them freely wander around the globe and truly become "the citizens of the world."

I have offered some random reflections on the possible direction for the task of globalization. But one thing is clear to me: these directions cannot be mapped out in detail before we actually embark on the task of globalization. Our direction will become clearer to us as we take the risk of globalizing theological education. It is the Abrahamic journey of faith that will lead us ultimately to the promised land of holistic theological education.

Notes

1. This is the predecessor to the present Program on Theological Education of the World Council of Churches. As TEF, it was mainly concerned with theological education in the Two-Thirds World. But now, as PTE, its work is extended to all the six continents.

2. Karl Barth, *Church Dogmatics*, I, 1., Edinburgh: T & T Clark, 1975, p. xvi.

TEACHING FOR ECUMENISM:

A Personal Journey

JANE CARY CHAPMAN PECK

Dr. Peck made the following presentation in Madison, Wisconsin, on March 23, 1990, having travelled from Nicaragua, where she and her husband were spending their sabbatical doing research and development work. Later that month she flew to Seoul, Korea, as a United Methodist delegate to the World Council of Churches Consultation on "Justice, Peace and the Integrity of Creation." From there she went directly to Uppsala, Sweden, for a meeting of the Life and Peace Institute, on which she served as a director. It was in early May, in Sweden, that she was hospitalized, and she returned immediately to the United States to began treatment for a malignancy. Jane Cary Peck died on September 10, 1990, at age 58. Earlier this year, she was awarded posthumously the 1991 New England United Methodist Award for Excellence in Social Justice Actions by the Southern New England Annual Conference.

Because her presentation was written under difficult circumstances in Nicaragua, Dr. Peck intended to revise it substantially. Unfortunately, her deteriorating health prevented her from carrying out this work. Following her death, I prepared the manuscript for publication, without, of course, the additional material that Dr. Peck would have included.--Jeanne Audrey Powers, Associate General Secretary, Commission on Christian Unity and Interreligious Concerns

Gleanings along an Ecumenical Journey

I have been asked to share with you the ways in which, as a United Methodist professor, I have found opportunities to incorporate an ecumenical perspective into my teaching of social ethics. I've also been asked to share ways in which I have familiarized my classes with national and international ecumenical agencies, resources, and persons of leadership in order that my students may use those sources in their future ministry. Finally, the planning committee asked me, "How did you get that way?" And that may be the hardest question of all!

The task, however, has given me a rich opportunity to reflect on how ecumenical elements have influenced my profession and brought me to this place. In that reflection on my own journey, I have become aware of how much ecumenical experience has blessed my life from the very beginning and in all its dimensions.

- I have experienced the global community of believers in ecumenical worship, in study, and in action/reflection within the institutional and denominational church and in many forms of councils of churches.

- I have been part of the one Body of Christ in its amazing many-splendored diversity-in-unity--and in its shameful, soul-wrenching, unfaithfulness and brokenness-in-disunity, along with its sometimes tedious plenaries, male-dominated small groups, and occasionally boring worship.

- I have experienced the spiritual and political power of the global ecumenical community in prophetic actions, in solidarity, and in sharing with interreligious Third World task forces and special delegations--one to El Salvador in a time of grave threat to the church and another to the five Central American presidents and National Commissions of Reconciliation on behalf of their Esquipulas Peace Plan.

- I have experienced ecumenical vitality, challenge, and nourishment in faith-based communities of justice, peacemaking, and sisterhood, transcending all boundaries and barriers. In these communities our common calling, passion, and commitment are celebrated in and fed by shared Eucharist, prayer, and rich engagement with Scripture and each other's life experience.

Professor Janice Love, a United Methodist member of the Central Committee of the World Council of Churches (WCC), sees the world as a "necrophilic system," founded on "materialism, Machiavellianism, militarism, and patriarchy.[1] It is ecumenical experience that has called me out of that system and into what Jose Miguez Bonino calls "the oikoumene of solidarity." This "oikoumene of solidarity" is an order of mutual support, common concern and suffering, and joint celebration and hope among solidarity organizations and churches of the North and South America and the world ecumenical movement. The radical faith of this movement is that "the reality of God is more decisive than the reality of the world as it is" and that the reality of God demands "transformation of understanding, repentance, and conversion." In this movement the poor and marginal--especially including, I would add, women and young people--are the human bearers of the miraculous possibility of change, their "hopeful suffering containing the possibility of a new and different oikoumene, of solidarity and life."[2] The oikoumene of solidarity is the foundation for my teaching of social ethics. It is also the vision for my ecumenical work and for global justice and peace in the Church, the seminary, and the world.

Personal Ecumenical Journey

It wasn't the most auspicious beginning for an ecumenical journey. I grew up in a small Georgia town of Methodists and Baptists, where the few Presbyterians were regarded as a kind of strange sect! But I was nurtured by a mother strongly influenced by her college experience in the YWCA with its global, ecumenical, and rich theological perspectives; and I was formed by the local Methodist Youth Fellowship, the North Georgia Conference's Camp Glisson, and by high school "Y" experiences. My Christian faith and vocational direction were influenced by my leadership in the YWCA of Wesleyan College (Georgia), with its international and interracial speakers and its Student Christian Movement conferences, as well as publications such as *motive* and *Concern*. In 1954, I attended the Evanston Assembly of the WCC as a Wesley Foundation director at Georgia State College for Women and Georgia Military College. In 1966, while I was a student at Boston University School of Theology, I took a course in ethics from Dean Walter C. Muelder, who was preparing to participate in the 1966 WCC Church and Society Conference held in Geneva. As I studied its four volumes of materials, I was led to my vocation as an ecumenical ethicist in theological education.

I am a member of the faculty at Andover Newton Theological School, an American Baptist and United Church of Christ seminary. A highly ecumenical seminary itself, it belongs to the Boston Theological Institute Ecumenical seminary consortium. For the thirteen years that I have taught at Andover Newton, I have been a member of the United Methodist delegation on the NCC Governing Board, serving this year as vice-president. My extensive involvement in the WCC as a United Methodist representative includes the 1979 Church and Society Conference on "Faith, Science, and the Future," held at MIT; a 1983 WCC pre-assembly delegation visitation to the churches in Cuba; the 1983 Sixth Assembly of the WCC held in Vancouver; plans to attend the upcoming 1991 Seventh Assembly of the WCC, to be held in Canberra, Australia; two emergency delegations to Central America, composed of representatives of the WCC, NCCC (National Council of the Churches of Christ), and the Latin American Council of Churches; and participation as a delegate to the 1990 WCC Convocation on "Justice, Peace, and the Integrity of Creation" in Seoul, Korea.

As a local church person serving on ecumenical bodies of the wider church, I am a lay member of my town's Ecumenical Association, composed of lay and clergy representatives from each church in Williamstown, Massachusetts. My ecumenical work has also included membership on the board of an international ecumenical peace research organization, the Life and Peace Institute, based in Uppsala, Sweden, and extensive work with Witness for Peace, a faith-based organization of U.S. citizens in solidarity with the people of Nicaragua.

United Methodist Faculty Leadership Involvement

I have shared this with you, at the planning committee's request, to indicate to you the ways in which my teaching and my commitments have arisen out of the context of this intentional ecumenical and global involvement.

Of course, I am not unique in this regard. The ecumenical movement depends on many persons whose "home base" is the theological seminary. Through their own ecumenical experiences, these persons have drawn inspiration, insights, and knowledge for teaching ecumenics. In so doing, they are helping to create an ecumenical ethos and global perspective in our seminaries. United Methodist seminary faculty members have contributed, and been enriched by, ecumenical experiences in the following ways:

- participation in WCC, NCCC, or the Consultation on Church Union (COCU) plenaries, meetings, and committees, as delegates, advisors, participant/observers, or stewards;

- as members of the Commission on Christian Unity and Interreligious Concerns (CCUIC), at the annual conference or general church level;

- within a local ecumenical organization, such as a council of churches or a clergy association;

- as consultants to an ecumenical agency or its task forces, or as speakers for special events;

- as members of ecumenical peace and justice advocacy groups on any number of specialized issues, many within an international context;

- as researchers in ecumenical studies (on theological issues or on the work of scholars from across the ecclesiological spectrum);

- as contributors to ecumenical publications, including: the New Revised Standard Version of the Bible; the Inclusive Language Lectionary; "Justice, Peace, and the Integrity of Creation" preparatory materials; NCCC studies of the Church and "Apostolic Faith," "Homosexuality," "The Community of Women and Men in the Church," and "Foundations for Ecumenical Commitment;" and Peace Research and Human Rights Advocacy;

- utilizing WCC and NCCC study books and resource materials;

- bringing ecumenical leaders to the seminary as speakers or preachers; and being such a speaker, with an explicitly ecumenical, interreligious, or international focus;

- developing a Visiting Scholar Program across national, denominational, or religious boundaries;

- participating in ecumenical groups, contributing United Methodist faculty publications and research.

There are other numerous ways in which such opportunities present themselves to faculty who are intentional about their ecumenical involvement for the sake of the seminary and the students they teach.

Using Ecumenical Resources in Theological Education

In my classes we try to develop among ourselves a learning community of mutual resourcing and enrichment, including searching and questioning. In this environment, we can intentionally work on developing and practicing the values of an ecumenical community. Students are expected to learn their own denominations' positions and resources--people and publications--on social issues and ecumenism and use them in class presentations and discussions.

Class discussions focus on special events in the lives of churches, such as the reunification of the Presbyterian Church, the 200th anniversary of the African Methodist Episcopal Church, and the decisions by the American Baptist Churches and the Evangelical Lutheran Church in America to reaffirm their memberships in the NCCC and the WCC. Once we had the opportunity to discuss the election of one of our class members as moderator of the United Church of Christ! We put emphasis on events within ecumenical bodies themselves, such as the WCC's Faith and Order Commission's development of the *Baptism, Eucharist and Ministry* (BEM) document and its accompanying "Lima Liturgy," bilateral dialogues between churches. We also take up issues of conflict, such as the application for membership in the NCCC by the Universal Fellowship of Metropolitan Community Churches, the *Reader's Digest-*"60 Minutes" furor, the WCC Programme to Combat Racism grants and program, the publication of the NCCC *Inclusive Language Lectionary*, among others. As a class, we struggle together on issues of unity and justice.

In any one of these issues, all the disciplines of theological study are present: Scripture, Church history, theology, ethics, communication, and so forth. Ecumenical issues, events, and resources provide superb content for an inductive method of teaching social ethics. A host of courses are possible with any combination of this subject matter. The World Council of Churches provides resources for and from major international gatherings, which often include media presentations, posters and packets, liturgies and prayers.

Spiritual Enrichment

Many ecumenical resources can be adapted for ongoing use. Let me give you a few examples:

Ecumenical worship resources have enriched the beginning of my classes. The worship book from the Sixth Assembly of the World Council, "Jesus Christ--the Life of the World," includes music, prayers, and litanies--all in at least four languages. Using a page that is multilingual reminds everyone that Christ is not captive to American church life and links us with the Christian communities in many cultures.

The Ecumenical Prayer Cycle, "With All God's People," is outlined into 52 sections for each week of the year. Each part of the world where Christian churches exist is lifted up with a simple map, a brief history of Christianity in that country or region, prayers from their churches' worship life, and a description of what issues Christians are struggling with there. These become part of each week's prayers. By the time students complete my class, they have an education in church life and devotion and an additional exposure to global Christian experience.

Each year the Consultation on Church Union, in cooperation with the three historically black Methodist churches, publishes a Lenten devotional booklet entitled, "Liberation and Unity." Students who use this booklet see Christian devotion from another perspective as they hear the salvation story expressed with a different cultural viewpoint.

These ecumenical resources have been used in student presentations and at times of celebration or sorrow in class. These materials integrate spirituality/worship, global and multiracial perspectives, Christian unity, and justice and peace concerns. Students who have been introduced to these ecumenical and global resources will widen their own horizons, and take this wider vision of the church into the congregations they will serve.

Specific Courses

Both the national and the World Council of Churches are deeply involved in issues of social justice, and because of this many of their conferences and background materials provide analyses of political, economic, and human rights issues. Because the World Council reflects the world's diversity, events and the preparatory materials frequently contain a unique, global perspective on such issues. This approach to questions of church in society can be quite different from anything students from the United States have seen before. The problems of hunger, militarism, family, war, and water (to mention just a few) sound new when they are formulated from another language base. Students may discover fresh areas of concern and sense the urgent need for solutions. Students who are exposed to different cultural patterns often find a totally different prism through which to see justice issues.

In the WCC area, phrases that have become important frequently represent major themes or emphases, and each of those have provided course titles: "Faith, Science, and the Future," "A Just, Participatory, Sustainable Society," "The Ecumenical Decade: Churches in Solidarity with Women," "Justice, Peace, and the Integrity of Creation," "Baptism, Eucharist and Ministry," and "Your Will Be Done: Mission in Christ's Way." An ample bibliography accompanies each class, and relevance continues long after the themes or conferences cease to be in the calendar. *Midstream, The Ecumenical Review,* and *The International al Review of Missions,* for example, are journals that offer commentary, dialogue, and response to these themes. Frequently, an article will summarize a series of responses. (For example, the responses to BEM alone have provided six successive volumes!)

Continuing with the WCC, the work of some of its units frequently disclose issues of conflict, autonomy, and authority, as well as biblical or theological insights. The controversial Programme to Combat Racism raises questions regarding marginal and radical organizations. When those occur in the United States, the students are confronted with justice-seeking groups they did not even know existed. Some students have chosen to do research on such groups, such as the Association of Haitian Workers, the Black Consciousness Movement, the Gathering of the Peoples Group (with the Anishinabe people), the Training and Research Institute on Migration. Each of these organizations opens up an extensive set of issues of justice, which can awaken students to the needs in their own country.

In the arena of the NCCC, policy statements or resolutions on Latin American issues frequently provide data for a course I teach on Latin American Liberation Ethics. The "Middle East Policy Statement" (a booklet in itself) summarizes the history of both Palestinian and Israeli relationships with the land, the origin of the state of Israel, the role of the Christian church, the issues of security, and human rights. Students using these materials as texts have a foundation not only for a more intelligent reading of the daily newspapers but also for the role of the Church in seeking to provide counsel to the communions regarding problems in these "holy lands."

When the NCCC was reviewing the application of the Universal Fellowship of Metropolitan Community Churches for membership in the NCCC, the papers developed by each of the communions describing their present formal stance toward homosexual persons provided a basis for analyzing the sources of authority in each of the communions, to say nothing about the host of perspectives on homosexual issues by NCCC member communions.

The historical records of both the World Council and the National Council of Churches have been my primary source when I teach a course on "The Social Teachings of the Church." Each class in "ecumenical ethics" gets firsthand experience with the organizations they have previously recognized only by name. A full day's field trip to the "God Box," as some of my students call 475 Riverside in New York City, includes a visit with top staff of the NCC and the U.S. Office of the World Council. Eight to ten persons either make presentations or are interviewed by students who have special interests in various elements of NCCC and WCC work. When issues and individuals are "personalized" in direct conversation, new learnings and new motivations become apparent in the final papers of the students.

The Seminary Bookstore and Library

As a faculty member, I review each year the new World Council and National Council materials with the head librarian and the manager of the seminary bookstore. Literature is extensive, and the WCC publishes an annotated booklet to update its list. This booklet allows us to find useful supplementary material according to the courses being offered each school year.

The library subscribes to all WCC publications and buys almost all of the books. It frequently has special displays during major ecumenical events. The bookstore stocks ecumenical resources beyond those required for courses, and it reviews some in the school newsletter. As an interested ecumenical faculty member, I distribute copies of the WCC publications booklet to the faculty each year.

When I teach, I am committed to raising up a new generation of seminary graduates (of whatever age) who see themselves participating in both the "re-forming" of the church and the creating of a just society. When the work of the academy is united with the life of the Church, I believe that a living reality is evoked within the Body of Christ.

Ecumenical Formation

The church urgently needs the formation and development of strong new ecumenical leadership for ecumenical bodies and our communions. With the changed age and experience composition of our seminary student bodies, those who need to be "evangelized" as new ecumenists will not be the usual "young people" (who might serve as stewards at international meetings) but rather second or third-career women and men. In that sense, it also becomes the responsibility of the local congregation to provide a place for ecumenical formation.

The great student ecumenical movement and its organizations are no more, but attempts are being made to recover the spirit of the older Inter-Seminary Movement. Perhaps the Women's Inter-Seminary (students) Conference, held annually, provides the closest student ecumenical experience of earlier days. Some seminaries have made a particular effort to see that there is student representation at WCC Assemblies, such as at Vancouver or Canberra, either as accredited visitors or as part of a seminary study-travel seminar (Claremont School of Theology offered credit for students from a number of different seminaries at each of these assemblies). Some denominational ecumenical offices have provided scholarships for particular ecumenical events, such as the annual National Workshop on Christian Unity or the Auburn Theological Seminary sponsored "Ecumenical Moment" in 1989, a ten-day period of "living-learning" exposure to ecumenical issues and leadership at the Stony Point, N.Y. Conference Center. But these events seem few and far between, and therefore the major responsibility still lies with the seminaries.

It is not uncommon that students who have attended ecumenical events become frustrated when they return to find so few student (and also faculty) colleagues willing to share their new visions. One way to cope with this problem has been to urge that at least two representatives (either student or faculty) participate in such events so that momentum at the seminary can be sustained. In some cases this has resulted in the formation of a student/faculty "Ecumenical Committee" and in applications for the Graduate Program in Ecumenical Studies at the Ecumenical Institute in Bossey, Switzerland. Students (and faculty who have accompanied them) have attended short courses or an exchange semester in the Third World, mostly Latin America or India, which has enriched our own community life on their return.

When I ask students to tell about their "ecumenical experience" at the beginning of some of my courses, the majority report only involvement in annual Thanksgiving or possibly World Day of Prayer ecumenical services. Very few can point to a great deal of involvement, knowledge, or interest in ecumenism by their home or field-education churches. Dr. Wesley Ariarajah, a Sri Lankan Methodist on the WCC staff, once told me a story that illustrates the difference local church involvement in ecumenical issues can make. His formation as an ecumenist, he said, took place because of the influence of his pastor, who reported to his congregation over the years on every ecumenical conference he prepared for and attended and informed them on the great ecumenical issues of the day. That pastor was Dr. D. T. Niles. At least two people who grew up in that church are on the Geneva WCC staff today, and I am sure that others from that congregation are making their ecumenical witness elsewhere. That is the kind of minister I passionately long for our seminaries to educate and nurture.

United Methodist Ecumenical Future

Despite our rich diversity of faculty and students (Protestant, Orthodox, Anglican, and Roman Catholic), we seldom intentionally tap that source in order to deepen the ecumenical movement. A faculty or student body that merely represents denominational loyalties does not an ecumenical seminary make! In most United Methodist seminaries there are very few courses explicitly related to ecumenics. Ecumenical consortiums look good on paper, but the field of ecumenism is rarely included in the crucial task of shaping a theological curriculum.

Ecumenism is our United Methodist heritage and commitment. Sometimes, because of our size and complex organization, I believe we do not notice other members of the Body of Christ. We expend our greatest time and energy on our own multiple organizational components, requirements, and resources. Seminary teaching, scholarship in our particular disciplines, and committee work are so demanding that we do not pay attention to the international ecumenical movement, including our own communion's role and contribution to the movement. Our seminaries may not take note of our bishops'--or conference lay people's--ecumenical involvement and leadership on vital ecumenical issues of the day. Seldom do we seminary faculty look upon ecumenics as a focus for our next research project or publication.

Here, therefore, is my "short list" of recommendations that I, as a United Methodist committed to theological education and to ecumenism, would make to our United Methodist seminaries and to our students:

(1) Inclusion of commitment to ecumenical and global theological education in any seminary mission statements or statements of purpose.

(2) Attention to ecumenical commitment in hiring regular and adjunct faculty, in inviting visiting scholars and campus speakers and preachers, and in designing and revising curriculum.

(3) Encouragement of ecumenical research and publication, with recognition and credit for ecumenical participation in promotion and tenure consideration.

(4) A comprehensive library and bookstore provision of ecumenical resources.

(5) A closer relationship between Conference Commissions on Christian Unity and Interreligious Concerns and seminaries within the conference.

(6) Specific invitations from seminaries to non-UM board members of NCCC or WCC units who live in the seminary area to speak or engage in informal conversations with students and faculty.

Conclusion

In the summer of 1986, the Ecumenical Institute in Bossey, Switzerland, and the Programme on Theological Education of the WCC sponsored a ten-day event entitled, "The Teaching of Ecumenics." A superb publication of the same name, containing the papers and recommendations from that conference, should be required reading for professors in any area of seminary education. One of the organizers of this conference, Dr. Daniel F. Martensen, writes about the vital need to teach ecumenics today:

Ecumenics deals with a unique body of material and insight produced by the modern ecumenical movement. This insight and documentation impinges upon the classical theological disciplines but has its own integrity. More importantly, *unless the question for Christian unity and common witness and service is addressed in concerted fashion and in self-consciously defined courses of study, the ecumenical memory, to say nothing of the ecumenical vision of the future, will be lost.*[3] (emphasis added)

I believe that we who are seminary faculty have a unique opportunity to sustain that memory, articulate that vision, and participate in the shaping of a new ecumenical generation. May that be our common vocation.

Notes

1. Janice Love, "The Necrophiliac System," in *Whither Ecumenism?* Thomas Wieser, ed. (Geneva: World Council of Churches, 1986), 31.

2. Jose Miguez Bonino, "Oikoumene and anti-Oikoumene," in *Whither Ecumenism?* 30.

3. In Samuel Amirtham and Cyris H.S. Moon, eds., *The Teaching of Ecumenics* (Geneva: World Council of Churches, 1987). This book is available through the Publications Department of the World Council (in the U.S., from the U.S. Office of the WCC, Room 915, New York, NY 10115-0050).

IMPLICATIONS OF THE YAHARA PAPERS FOR SEMINARIES AND FOR THEOLOGICAL EDUCATION

RIDGWAY F. SHINN,JR.,
& NORMAN E. DEWIRE

Volume eleven of *Quarterly Review* carried several of the papers presented at the Yahara Consultation of March 1990. In view of the numerous ideas and concerns raised in those papers, it seems reasonable at this juncture to ask, What may one make of them? Can one find substantive matters to be learned and applied to seminaries specifically, and to theological education more broadly?

Perhaps the major insight from the collected papers is that they come at a strategic time in theological education. The Association of Theological Schools' work on globalization has influenced faculty and administrators in all seminaries, including those related to The United Methodist Church. They call for theological reflection, especially in light of the official responses from the churches to *Baptism, Eucharist, and Ministry*, the document which sets out what some believe to be the most significant ecumenical convergence of this century. Moreover, seminaries must respond to the increasing reality of other living faiths emerging in significant ways on the U.S. religious scene. The increasing interest in spiritual formation also calls for a response from seminaries.

The Yahara papers cumulatively and collectively lead to a *gestalt*, that is, a persuasive and powerful insight ineluctably rooted in the totality. They proclaim a vision of an ecumenically renewed and reconstructed theological education, radically transformed in faithfulness to the ongoing search to understand the nature of God and to comprehend God's action in Christ. Theological educators should not merely "tinker" with components, to add a course here and there or to arrange a short-term visit, but rather they are called to reconceive, re-envision, and redirect the whole enterprise!

The Yahara Consultation was also the setting for some vital but unpublished scholarly work. The members of the consultation were divided into six working groups, each of which focused on a specific

127

issue: Ecclesial Agreements: Reception in Church and Seminary; Denominational Formation and Ecumenical Formation; Developing the Next Generation of Ecumenical Leadership; Ministerial Formation in an Increasingly Interreligious Context; The Terminology of Unity: Meanings, Relationships, Conflicts, and Priorities; Theological Import and Adequacy of "Globalization." By the end of the consultation, each working group drafted a substantive and suggestive paper which included reflection on the formal papers presented as well as the shared knowledge, experience, and wisdom of the participants. This essay draws upon both the papers as published and the writers' access to other work accomplished at Yahara.

From all those materials, numerous clues and strands intertwine to suggest possible directions for transformation. From these we have isolated five themes that may well indicate the direction of theological education in the future:

- theological education is broader than seminary education;
- United Methodist identity is constitutively defined to include ecumenism;
- both confession and passion are needed in relation to ecumenism;
- tension points require explicit attention, not avoidance;
- interreligious dialogue is critical and essential, especially to address justice issues among the human family.

Seminary Education as Part of Theological Education

While seminaries are a critical locus for theological education, theological education is broader than seminary degrees. The concept of theological education must include the entire spectrum of *laos*, that is, all baptized Christians, the overwhelming number of whom will never seek seminary degrees. From that number, certain vitally important persons will respond to God's call and seek preparation for representative ministries through seminaries. Theological education also includes those persons already within representative ministry, who have insights and learnings to share. Roy Sano's plea for addressing the intradenominational tension between liberals and evangelicals of The United Methodist Church requires a vision of theological education that goes beyond seminary bounds.[1] The task of reordering the life, ethos, and offerings of the seminary is sufficiently staggering but even that is not enough. For example, Loren Mead of the Alban Institute

128

foresees every local congregation functioning as a kind of seminary: "Not the ones we've known, but a reinvented seminary. The ones we have train a professional cadre in three years. The ones we need are life-long centers of training, retraining, and nurture."[2]

For the vision of households, the *oikos*, which Douglas Meeks sketched[3] and for the understanding of the "three tables" which Russell Richey described[4] to become incarnate in the conscious life and witness of baptized persons in congregations, we need the most comprehensive view of theological education.

Yet, within that comprehensive view there remains a critical, central place for the seminary. The Church must look there, primarily, for theologians to name the fundamental questions about God, Jesus Christ, and the world. The church must expect and support scholarship in all the areas that presently exist within seminaries. But seminaries also need to engage in the world, even at risk. Seminaries are called to be prophetic. The seminary curriculum, therefore, has accountability to the faith, to specific institutional missions, to the academy, and to the wider world. The Church needs all the expertise it can assemble to prepare persons for ordained and consecrated ministries. This must be done from the intertwined perspectives of globalization, ecumenism, and interreligious dialogue.[5]

Ecumenism and the Denomination

For United Methodists both denominationalism and ecumenism are important. Several authors[6] call attention to the ecumenical stance of The United Methodist Church, which embeds these words in the Preamble to its Constitution:

The Church of Jesus Christ exists in and for the world, and its very dividedness is a hindrance to its mission in that world.

John Deschner arged that ecumenism "is not an extra, but is essential and constitutive for United Methodism as a church." If, as he continues, ecumenism goes beyond its concern for the dividedness of the Church (important as that is) and attempts to heal the brokenness of the human community, then Methodism and ecumenism become inextricably linked. "No 'distinctives,' no United Methodists...no ecumenical commitment, no United Methodists either...."[7] Deschner concludes that United Methodists should recast theological education, in light of Wesley's understanding of grace.[8] Such recasting must maintain a concern for Methodist distinctiveness and particularity, but only within the broader context of ecumenical commitment. Both must be done simultaneously. Certainly, this implication requires careful and thoughtful attention.

A Passion for Ecumenism

At present, United Methodists seem unwilling or unable to confess their part in perpetuating the dividedness of the Church and evidence little passion for ecumenism.[9] Perhaps the most telling comment is that of Michael Kinnamon:

I speak as a person who loves the United Methodist Church when I say that the biggest objection I hear from your--our--ecumenical partners is that the Methodists are too self-sufficient.[10]

Have United Methodists outgrown ecumenism? Do United Methodists worry more about denominational survival and declining membership than they do about the dividedness of the Church? Are United Methodists unwilling to envision the coming great Church if it is not precisely like the present, or even any, institutional church? It appears that United Methodists are turning their collective backs, and minds, on John Deschner's point: the centrality of ecumenism as constitutive for United Methodists' self-understanding.

Inclusive church unity is constitutive for United Methodism--as constitutive as personal sanctification is for Wesleyan salvation. United Methodism has its being, its integrity, only in relation to the whole church of Christ. We cannot be ourselves without being ecumenical. That is what Wesley saw in his construal of the relation of the Methodists to the Church of England. And it remains utterly clear in principle in the Constitution and Discipline of our denomination.[11]

United Methodist-related seminaries can lead United Methodists to understand the centrality of ecumenism and commit themselves passionately to it. Other denominations' seminaries have recently experienced pressure from persons seeking to enforce "doctrinal conformity"; this may well be coming to United Methodist-related seminaries. James V. Heidinger, II, in *Good News* identifies this issue for attention at the 1992 General Conference:

3. Call seminaries to theological accountability. Many of us wonder if our seminaries have become such handmaidens to America's secular universities that they've lost all sense of accountability to the church. Who oversees the doctrinal integrity of our UM theological seminaries?...Whose job is it to guarantee that our denominational seminaries are teaching theology which faithfully reflects United Methodist doctrine as outlined in the *Book of Dis-*

cipline? Isn't it time the church called our seminaries to doctrinal account-ability?[12]

This appears to be a call, not to ecumenism and denominationalism together, but to United Methodist particularism. Roy Sano notes the need for "a much sharper focus on the tension between evangelicals and liberals within The United Methodist Church."[13] And that will most certainly include tension around the foci of theological education.

The lack of confession and passion are of serious concern. Theological education, as all education, is committed to the ongoing search for truth. But this includes the potential of new truth breaking in and being found, and especially truth about the nature of God, and for this both confession and passion are needed. If theological education is to reflect the *gestalt* of interweaving ecumenism, globalization, and interreligious dialogue, it seems essential that we lament the brokenness of the Church and feel the pains of division. There can be no "mutually vulnerable pursuit of truth" without that foundation.[14]

Difficult Areas for Future Debate

Vital issues are at stake here not only for theological education but also for the faith itself. Simply to avoid tangling with the issues and to choose an "opting-out" stance will do a profound disservice to theological education.

What is the stance for addressing such issues? Again the phrase was introduced by Michael Kinnamon: the "mutually vulnerable pursuit of truth."[15] That is a taut phrase with profound meaning. Participants need to begin their study with questions rather than declarations, with hypotheses rather than conclusions, with open minds rather than closed minds, with a deep commitment to searching for truth whether old or new rather than simply restating given positions. Should participants enter such study with the assumption that truth is finite and fully known, the opportunity for substantive theological reflection will be lost. The question of stance with its methodological implications is the first area needing debate and resolution.

What are some of the critical areas of tension raised in these papers? They are numerous, to be sure. We are making no attempt to develop a comprehensive listing but rather to identify some of the areas that seem worthy of careful study.

1. Defining the Terms

First, there is a clear need to develop a working understanding of the three terms that played such a large part in the Yahara papers: globalization, ecumenism, and interreligious dialogue. It is possible that this may be best done by assuming that all three are essential to theological education. The practical work toward implementing them may be far preferable to the abstract exercise of defining them. Whatever the approach, there is a substantial body of work to be done around these three key terms.[16]

Indeed, the term ecumenism moves in two related directions. There is the three-level meaning many would recognize. The term ecumenism refers: "1) to unity and renewal of the whole Christian community...; 2) to the world-wide mission of the church, and 3) to the unity of the whole human family."[17] On the other hand, Douglas Meeks goes to the root word, *oikos*, household or home, and suggests a different set of meanings: the relationship between economy, ecology, and *oikoumene*. He writes:

The question of economy is, will everyone in the household have access to what it takes to live and live abundantly? The question of ecology is, will nature have a home, its own living space? The question of *oikoumene* is, will the peoples of the earth be able to inhabit the world in peace? Taken together they constitute *oikoumene* as the most comprehensive horizon for the church's service of God's redemption of the world.[18]

It is worth recalling Diedra Kriewald's point that many church leaders "operate from a denominational perspective that rarely includes the language or root metaphors of ecumenism."[19] Certainly, once these sets of meanings are studied and understood, more will be necessary to move them into the conscious and subconscious thought patterns of church folk.

2. Mission and Witness

Another area that calls for attention is the ongoing relationship between Christian mission and witness (which also have multiple meanings) and global mutuality and solidarity. That means more than simply a "sending" side to the equation; it calls for theological reflection and human interaction among diverse peoples and cultures.[20] It calls for further work on the relationships between particularity and wholeness, to say nothing of the entire issue of contextualization.[21]

An observation made by Lamin Sanneh needs substantial review: "We need to be aware of the fact that all religious claims are intended for human custody even where they direct us to transcendent ends."[22] While his comment was directed to Muslim-Christian relationships, it is an important point upon which to reflect. It moves beyond a merely "comparative religions" view and presses to a differing understanding of the reality of God's creation.

3. The Teaching Office

Another interesting concern raised has to do with the location of the magisterium, or teaching office. One thinks of the ways in which the Council of Bishops has exercised its teaching office through two important initiatives: *In Defense of Creation* and *Vital Congregations: Faithful Disciples*. But in United Methodist polity, the General Conference is ultimate. John Deschner has raised the possibility that United Methodism may be responding to a growing conciliar magisterium and asked whether that is a direction that should be encouraged and supported. In a fascinating analysis, he described the process by which The United Methodist Church fashioned its response to that critical document from the World Council of Churches, *Baptism, Eucharist, and Ministry*.[23] There, the General Conference delegated the task of response to the Council of Bishops. While that is significant in itself, his principal point was that, in asking vital questions and in receiving responses from 189 churches, the World Council of Churches, in effect, was itself exercising the teaching office. Certainly the whole question of teaching office, and the role of seminaries in that, requires exploration.

4. A New Pedagogy

Pedagogy, that is, the selection and focus of content, the rationale, perspectives, and assumptions for curriculum and courses, and the actual mode of instruction, is integral to any educational process. Closely related, of course, is what experience, perspectives, scholarship, and preparation seminary faculty and other teachers need. For example, Thomas Thangaraj is explicit in his recommendation:

We need to adopt an entirely different theological and educational methodology in all the courses that are taught in our schools. Each subject that is offered in the seminary or school should be taught in such a way that the global-contextual matrix of that particular discipline is highlighted and explicated.[24]

Jane Cary Peck described, in considerable detail, the ways in which she, as a seminary professor, used ecumenical resources and perspectives. In each class, she used a searching, questioning mode of instruction so that "In this environment, we can intentionally work on developing and practicing the values of an ecumenical community."[25] The seminary class itself, therefore, became not only an academic experience but also an ecumenical one. Diedra Kriewald calls on The United Methodist Church to tap the research and writing resources assembled in the seminaries for the issues of ecumenism and to recognize that: "the seminary communities can become centers of information and interpretation to help restore balance and discourage litmus testing...."[26]

These, then, are some of the issues which will create tension and conflict but which require study and addressing so that theological education can change as it needs to.

Dialogue and Global Justice

The more encompassing meaning of ecumenism or the threefold meaning rooted in *oikos* is in many ways the most complex of the strands. It reflects a theological cutting edge; even to state it challenges some traditional Western notions about Christian mission.

This theme has a special urgency for Americans. U.S. society, in the past generation, has undergone radical changes, a trend that will almost certainly continue. By the turn of the century, for example, there will be more Muslims in this country than Jews. Every major city in this country encompasses a wide mix of persons from every part of the world, reflecting differing cultures, languages, and religions. As a society, we seem ill-equipped to comprehend such drastic change. The consciousness of being one world, sharing in "spaceship earth," and the interdependence of ecological systems are beginning to dominate our awareness. In religious circles the dialogue among Jews and Christians since the end of World War II has had a special common focus in trying to comprehend the Holocaust. Models for Muslim-Christian or Buddhist-Christian or Taoist-Christian or Shinto-Christian or Hindu-Christian relationships and dialogues lack the commonalities that seem to be found readily in Jewish-Christian dialogue.

What about the traditional understanding of missions from Christian churches in the Western world to non-Christians, which was stated succintly in the words of the "Great Commandment?" As many persons in the two-thirds world testify, it was not only Christ but Western culture that accompanied missionaries. Differing forms of witness and mission are now required. Authentic dialogue emerges as a new alternative that rests on a significant theological premise:

If dialogue is defined as a mutually vulnerable pursuit of truth..., then Christians can presumably learn something new about the nature and purpose of God from such encounters. The clear implication is that God is at work redemptively in and through these other communities (whose members we regard more as partners in God's work of shalom than as objects of conversion)....[27]

That premise, to be sure, is unacceptable to many Christians. If God is at work in all of the creation and among all the peoples of the world, how can we understand that reality in relation to the billions of people who are neither Jews nor Christians? Herein lies the need for dialogue and search.

Throughout the Yahara papers, there is high concurrence that the matter of interreligious dialogue must be addressed, that it is essential to globalization and to ecumenism, and that it is not optional. Jane Smith wrote out of her scholarly study and her direct experience with Muslim-Christian dialogue; Lamin Sanneh wrote out of his experience of conversion from Islam to Christianity; Thomas Thangaraj wrote out of his experiences in India and the West; Douglas Meeks, in the concluding paper at Yahara, lifted the broadest meanings out of the household of the human family.[28]

It is important that Christians engaged in dialogue commit themselves to the mutual search for truth and for knowledge about God. Second, Christians need a clear understanding of who they are, of what they believe, and of how they have experienced God's action through Jesus Christ, and reflected upon that. The particularity, "the specificity and concreteness of the human situation," of those in dialogue is vital to its success.[29] Third, it is essential to realize that all Christianity is contextual. Christianity has not only adapted as an institution, it has also borrowed from institutions. Fourth, persons in dialogue need to struggle with nuances of language. Finally, it may well be that human suffering is the common ground which authenticates dialogue, the reality that negates relativism, and the focus that requires human beings to join together to seek justice, as Douglas Meeks has argued.

Human suffering is a central problem in all religions. Each confronts the sufferings of humanity and the need to put an end to godless and inhuman relations of the world. The primary components of the religions' community of suffering are compassion, justice, and peace.[30]

Since there seems an endless amount of injustice and suffering around the world, there is some urgency in moving toward developing models for interreligious dialogue and incorporating them into theological education.

A Challenge for Leadership

Tranforming theological education will require leadership from a wide spectrum of persons in seminaries--deans, presidents, trustees, faculty, and students--as well as from agencies in The United Methodist Church, such as the General Commission on Christian Unity and Interreligious Concerns, the General Board of Higher Education and Ministry with its divisions, and the General Board of Discipleship with its publication programs and its work with laity. Clearly, there is a place for the Council of Bishops to continue with their initiatives and join in addressing some of these transformations in theological education. And, it must be pointed out, funding will be necessary to support some persons in research, study, conferencing, writing, and the like.

The tasks are formidable, especially since numerous pressing questions were *not* dealt with in the Yahara papers or any of the essays in this collection. Consider, for example, two clusters of questions:

The first: How would a local church or local congregation look after the transformation of theological education suggested in these papers comes into effect? This is the arena, perhaps, where denominational particularism might be expected to be strongest. Yet, in community after community, local congregations join together in informal and formal structures across wide denominational and interreligious boundaries to engage in collective acts of mercy, witness, and justice. Could it be that some congregations and local religious communities are already engaged in re-envisioning and redesigning? That is a possibility. But, it is also possible that denominational particularism may be the more stubborn reality when profound change is called for, especially in view of the enormous investment which local congregations have in plant and facilities. The local congregations will be different, but what will it be like?

The second: How will we carry out the theological task of seeking to understand all living faiths in relation to God's creation? That question, for some persons, cannot be raised because of their understanding of God's specific actions in Judeo-Christian history. Yet, if God is greater than a tribal deity, the question requires examination and study. At one level, this question might suggest the relativizing all religious views. Christians, by their name and understanding, see God's action most clearly in Christ. Yet, such claims become a barrier to any common search for God's actions.

The challenge of all this was well stated by Douglas Meeks in the concluding portion of his essay:

The ecumenical movement has also reminded us that the root of oppression is not just unjust structures but sin, which can only be healed in the koinonia created by God's grace. Therefore, that oneness of community is the means to mission. Nothing changes for the good in history without living relationship in dialogue, continuing conversation, face-to-face reciprocity, community of shared suffering working for justice. Life in fellowship, life in dialogue changes the atmosphere. ...But this means, above all, our own transformation: spiritually, socially, and economically.[31]

It is hoped that all those engaged in theological education will be prepared to take the risks of transforming the enterprise. Such transformation must be undertaken in faithfulness to beliefs and claims about the nature of God and with a clear understanding of God's action in Christ which, in all ways, seems the vital reality with which to enter the next steps.

Notes

1. Roy Sano, "Ecumenical and Interreligious Agenda of The United Methodist Church," *Quarterly Review* (Spring 1991): 91-2 (- Chapter 3, "The Church and the World: Ecumenical and Interreligious Agenda of The United Methodist Church,").

2. Loren Mead, "Re: Every Congregation a Seminary," mimeographed paper, Alban Institute, 1991.

3. Douglas Meeks, "Globalization and the *Oikumene* in Theological Education," *Quarterly Review 11/4* (Winter 1991): 68-85 (- Chapter 1, "Globalization and the *Oikoumene* in Theological Education,).

4. Russell Richey, "Three Ecumenical Agendas: A Methodist Perspective," *Quarterly Review* 11/4 (Winter 1991) 52-67 (- Chapter 2, "Family Meal, Holy Communion, and Love Feast: Three Ecumenical Metaphors,").

5. This is the point which Meeks stressed so strongly in the essay "Globalization and the *Oikumene* in Theological Education."

6. Sano, "Ecumenical Agenda," p. 83; Jane Cary Peck, "The United Methodist Agenda: Teaching for Ecumenism," *Quarterly Review* 11/3 (Fall, 1991): 77-81 (- Chapter 10, "Teaching for Ecumenism: A Personal Journey,"). Diedra Kriewald, "Theological Education in The United Methodist Church in Light of the Consultation on Church Union," *Quarterly Review* 11/3 (Fall 1991): 58-70 (- Chapter 7, "Theological Education in Light of the Consultation on Church Union,").

7. John Deschner, "United Methodism's Basic Ecumenical Policy," *Quarterly Review* 11/3 (Fall 1991). (- Chapter 4, "United Methodism's Basic Ecumenical Policy").

8. Deschner, "Basic Ecumenical Policy," p. 45; see also, Peck, "Teaching for Ecumenism," pp. 83-84; "Theological Education in Light of COCU," pp. 66-68.

9. For example, Russell Richey, "Findings and Observations from the 1978-88 Survey of United Methodist Seminaries," *Quarterly Review* 11/1 (Spring 1991 - Appendix 2 Chapter 5,) "Cultivating) the Passion for Unity: Four Key issues in the Globalization of Theological Education,") 65-6; Michael Kinnamon, "Naming the Issues in Ecumenical Perspectives and Interreligious Dialogue," *Quarterly Review* 11/1 (Spring 1991): 80; Sano, "Ecumenical Agenda," p. 83; Deschner, "Basic Ecumenical Policy," pp. 41-57.

10. Kinnamon, "Naming the Issues," p. 80.

11. Deschner, "Basic Ecumenical Policy,"; reread Kriewald, "Theological Education in Light of COCU," pp. 58-60, and ponder that experience.

12. James V. Heidinger, II, "Ten Key Issues at Next General Conference," *Good News* (January/February 1991), 18.

13. Sano, "Ecumenical Agenda," p. 91.

14. Kinnamon, "Naming the Issues," p. 78.

15. Kinnamon, "Naming the Issues," p. 78.

16. Richey, "Findings," pp. 64-5.

17. Kinnamon, "Naming the Issues," p. 71.

18. Meeks, "Globalization and the *Oikumene*," p. 72.

19. Kriewald, "Theological Education in Light of COCU," p. 60.

20. Jane I. Smith, "Implications for Interreligious Dialogue and Ecumenical Understanding," *Quarterly Review* 11/2 (Summer 1991): 71-2 (- Chapter 6, "The Terminology of Ecumenism and Interreligious Dialogue in Theological Education,").

21. Thomas Thangaraj, "The Global-Contextual Matrix in the Seminary Classroom," *Quarterly Review* 11/2 (Summer 1991): 76-9 ("The Global Contextual Matrix in the Seminary Classroom.".

22. Lamin Sanneh, "Religious Particularity in Muslim-Christian Dialogue," *Quarterly Review* 11/2 (Summer 1991): 50.

23. Deschner, "Basic Ecumenical Policy," pp. 53-55; see also Kriewald, "Theological Education in Light of COCU," pp. 66-68; and note her observation: "The teaching office to which we all attend is located somewhere in the structures of ecumenical dialogues," (p. 67).

24. Thangaraj, "The Global-Contextual Matrix," pp. 76-9.

25. Peck, "Teaching for Ecumenism," p. 77.

26. Kriewald, "Theological Education in Light of COCU," p. 64.

27. Kinnamon, "Naming the Issues," pp. 78-9; see also Sano, "United Methodist Agenda," p. 90: "At the same time, to say the obvious, there are persons best explained by Hinduism, Buddhism, Confucianism, Taoism, and

Shintoism, to mention the more conspicuous Asian traditions where more than half of humankind lives."

28. For each of the authors see throughout their essays as cited: Smith, pp. 61ff; Thangaraj, pp. 76ff; Meeks, pp. 71ff.

29. Sanneh, "Muslim-Christian Dialogue," p. 45.

30. Meeks, "Ecumenism and the *Oikumene*," p. 80.

31. Meeks, "Ecumenism and the *Oikumene*," p. 81.

APPENDIX 1

Participants in the Consultation on Ecumenical Perspectives and Interreligious Dialogue in Theological Education

YAHARA RETREAT CENTER
MADISON, WISCONSIN
MARCH 22-25, 1990

Dr. John Berthrong, Boston University School of Theology
Dr. Jose Ignacio Cabezon, Iliff School of Theology
Dr. Young Ho Chun, Saint Paul School of Theology
Dr. Melva W. Costen, Gammon Theological Seminary (Interdenomenational Theological Center)
Dr. John Deschner, Perkins School of Theology, Southern Methodist University
Dr. Norman Dewire, Methodist Theological School of Theology
The Rev. Patricia Ferris, Commission on Christian Unity and Interreligious Concerns
Dr. Thomas Frank, Candler School of Theology, Emory University
Dr. Alan Geyer, Wesley Theological Seminary
Bishop William B. Grove, President, General Commision on Christian Unity and Interreligious Concerns
Dr. Luke Harkey, Boston University School of Theology
Dr. Paul Jones, Saint Paul School of Theology
Dr. Michael Kinnamon, Lexington Theological Seminary
The Rev. Robert Kohler, Board of Higher Education and Ministry, Division of Ordained Ministry
Dr. Diedra Kriewald, Wesley Theological Seminary
Dr. Jung Young Lee, Drew University, The Divinity School
Dr. Douglass Lewis, Wesley Theological Seminary
Bishop William B. Lewis
Dr. Temba Mafico, Gammon Theological Seminary (Interdenomination Theological Center)
Dr. Kendall K. McCabe, United Theological Seminary
Dr. Douglas Meeks, Eden Theological Seminary
Dr. Donald E. Messer, Iliff School of Theology
Dr. Jean Miller Schmidt, Iliff School of Theology

Dr. Mary Elizabeth Moore, School of Theology at Claremont
Bishop William B. Oden
Dr. Michael Pappas, Holy Cross Theological Seminary
Dr. Jane Cary Peck, Andover-Newton Theological School
Dr. Jeanne Audrey Powers, Commission on Church Unity and Inter-religious Concerns
Dr. Stephen Rasor, Gammon Theological Seminary (Interdenominational Theological Center)
Dr. Robert Reber, Auburn Theological Seminary
Dr. Russell Richey, Duke University, The Divinity School
Dr. Sharon Ringe, Methodist Theological School in Ohio
The Rev. Dr. Bruce Robbins, General Commission on Church Unity and Interreligious Concerns
Dr. Cornish Rogers, School of Theology at Claremont
Dr. Lamin Sanneh, Yale University Divinity School
Bishop Roy I. Sano, United Methodist Church, Rocky Mountain Area
Ms. Carolyn Scavella, World Council of Churches
Dr. Ridgway Shinn, Jr., Commission on Christian Unity and Inter-religious Concerns
Dr. Jane I. Smith, Iliff School of Theology
Dr. Thomas Starnes, Board of Higher Education and Ministry, Division of Ordained Ministry
Dr. Fred Streng, Perkins School of Theology, Southern Methodist University
Dr. Edwin E. Sylvest, Jr., Perkins School of Theology, Southern Methodist University
Dr. Thomas Thangaraj, Candler School of Theology, Emory University
Dr. Richard Tholin, Garrett-Evangelical Theological Seminary
Dr. Norman E. Thomas, United Theological Seminary
Dr. Nehemiah Thompson, Commission on Christian Unity and Inter-religious Concerns
Dr. Fred Tiffany, Methodist Theological School in Ohio
Dr. Donald Treese, Board of Higher Education and Ministry, Division of Ordained Ministry
Dr. Paul Van Buren, Board of Higher Education and Ministry, Division of Diaconal Ministry
Dr. James Will, Garrett-Evangelical Theological Seminary
The Rev. Rebecca Youngblood, Board of Higher Education and Ministry, Division of Ordained Ministry

APPENDIX 2

Findings and Observations from the 1987-88
Survey of United Methodist Seminaries

RUSSELL E. RICHEY AND JEAN MILLER SCHMIDT

Across North American theological education something of a revolution is taking place. Its watchword is globalization. In its name, faculties revamp curricula to mandate courses on the third world, other living faiths, contextual theologies; schools seek exchange programs with and exposure experiences in third world churches for their students; administrators scurry around applying for grants to underwrite both faculty and student travel; faculty members engage in new dialogues or refurbish old ones; faculties pledge themselves to incorporate the perspectives thus gained in the core curriculum; the accrediting agency, The Association of Theological Schools in the United States and Canada (ATS), assesses battle readiness, maps grand strategies, trains leadership, recruits (through start-up funds), and moves toward making globalization a criterion for accreditation; schools revise their catalogs and promotional material to hoist this new banner as their own.

The new watchword does not exactly replace old battle cries--ecumenism, evangelism, world Christianity, missions, world religions. Rather, it envelops them. Yet, the place of these older notions of the church's and the seminary's larger horizons within the new campaign for globalization remains uncertain. The term 'globalization' invites schools to rethink the purpose of their work, to reorder priorities, to reconceive what students must learn and how they learn it, and so to reshape the leadership of the church. In this essay, we will provide some indication of how United Methodist schools are conceiving globalization--we should say, "were"--because our findings are already dated by recent curricular efforts at globalization in several of the schools.

Background to the Survey

In late 1987 and early 1988, Jean Miller Schmidt and Russell Richey, faculty members of Iliff and Duke respectively, surveyed the United

Methodist Seminaries on behalf of the Committee on Ecumenical Perspectives and Interreligious Dialogue in Theological Education of the General Commission on Christian Unity and Interreligious Concerns (GCCUIC) and the Division of Ordained Ministry (DOM) and the Association of United Methodist Theological Schools (AUMTS). This survey had been prompted by an earlier report that Richey and Schmidt made to GCCUIC on ecumenical and global developments in United Methodist seminaries, a report based entirely on their analysis of the schools' catalogs. Their report concluded by asking what role GCCUIC might/should play in the seminaries' thinking and planning about global and ecumenical factors and how the seminaries might/should, in turn, resource GCCUIC.

A mischievous query of this sort often catches the perpetrators rather than the intended victims. Richey and Schmidt found them-selves members of a new committee, the Committee on Ecumenical Perspectives and Interreligious Dialogue in Theological Education of GCCUIC. This committee, established at the March 1987 meeting of the commission, was charged to "work with seminaries on the place of ecumenical perspectives and interreligious dialogue in theological education." Chaired by Dr. Ridgway F. Shinn, Jr., a director of GCCUIC, and staffed by Associate General Secretary Jeanne Audrey Powers, this committee was comprised of directors of GCCUIC and DOM and seminary representatives. It initially included Bishop Melvin C. Talbert, Professor Harriet Miller of United Theological Seminary, Dr. Robert Reber of Auburn Seminary, lay representative Martha Watanabe, the Rev. Thomas Starnes from DOM, as well as Schmidt and Richey. (In the new quadrennium GCCUIC members Talbert, Miller, and Watanabe went off and Bishop William Oden, President Norman E. DeWire (METHESCO), the Rev. Patricia Farris and lay representative (and doctoral candidate) Carol Colley were appointed. The other members continued.) The committee took its first duty to be a more thorough survey of the ecumenical and interreligious interests and investments of the United Methodist theological schools. A questionnaire emerged from several committee sessions, went through numerous 'perfections', and was submitted to executive officers of both DOM and GCCUIC. In its final form, it sought information from the seminaries on the global, interreligious and ecumenical flavor of the entire scope of their operations:

the number and frequency of courses on ecumenical and interreligious topics;

whether global concerns claimed a central place in the curriculum, particularly in foundational courses;

how exchange programs, consortia, visiting lectureships and local dialogues claimed student attention;

faculty leadership in ecumenical and interreligious affairs;

the ecumenical dimension to worship and daily life;

the diversity (denominational, racial, national) of the student body and how that diversity is used;

the place of ecumenism in continuing education;

initiatives taken in response to the ATS emphasis on globalization; and future plans.

The survey invited attachments, copies of relevant reports and statistical data so that each school could present its ecumenical character to best advantage.

The Survey

The four-page instrument was sent to the dean or president of each school. Along with it went a covering letter from General Secretary the Rev. Dr. Robert W. Huston explaining that the survey was undertaken on behalf of AUMTS and DOM/BHEM. Follow-up letters were sent by Jeanne Audrey Powers as needed. All seminaries eventually reported except Gammon. Richey and Schmidt then digested the responses, put the information from the several schools into a common format, returned this overview to the seminaries for comment and correction, and corrected the draft as appropriate. The revised digest was reviewed by the GCCUIC committee, circulated to the seminaries and submitted to GCCUIC and DOM.

As the following commentary makes clear, the digest ought to be significant to both GCCUIC and DOM, particularly the former, for the detailed information it offers on the seminaries' ecumenical operations and actors. Because of its detail, the way that current developments have quickly dated it, and its lack of an analytical dimension, the committee found itself pushing beyond the survey to interpret its findings.

Summary Findings and Issues Raised

The survey represents a 1987-88 self-portrait of United Methodist seminary ecumenical and interreligious involvement. So understood, it provides a benchmark, a measure of the ecumenical character of seminary ethos, curriculum, and program.

1) Global Commitments. Seminaries are in curricular ferment and change, particularly in relation to the global, ecumenical or interreligious dimension of their life. Much of it seems to be the direct result of the Association of Theological Schools' (ATS) exploration of globaliza-

tion as a defining aspect of theological education, though in one or two instances long-standing world Christianity or ecumenical commitments seem operative. The institutional support for such global interests is hard to gauge but apparently growing. We infer from the tenor and scope of the reports clear, though not necessarily formal and official, commitment to globalization.

Most schools require at least one course that has high ecumenical or interreligious content and offer an array of electives with which to pursue those interests. The global, interreligious, or ecumenical flavor of the schools as a whole is impressive. That had been clear from the schools' catalogs; it was even more obvious, detailed, and concrete in their reports.

The survey disclosed within United Methodist seminaries a rich and complex array of concern, interest, involvement, activity, and program in the general arena described by such terms as ecumenical, global, interreligious, missional, international, third world. However, while the schools all claimed a global agenda, they differed in its conception and in the place accorded it (on these divergencies see below). The fact of this global concern will not surprise anyone presently working within theological education. We think it worth calling to the attention of the larger constituencies who have a vital concern for theological education and its products. Globalization is very much in vogue.

2) Faculty. Of particular note are the many faculty members whom the schools identify as possessing global interests. Some have long played ecumenical leadership roles. Others represent new talent on which GCCUIC and other agencies of the church may wish to call. Of special note on these 'ecumenical lists' are the non-Methodists serving on United Methodist seminary faculties, a talent pool not now well utilized by United Methodism. Here we would point to a larger issue, one raised for GCCUIC by the disclosure of this global talent, but with ramifications for the entire church. How should the church make use of its intellectual capital, in this instance, that represented on seminary faculties? And has it been well used in the recent past? We think not. Seminary faculty participation in boards and agencies seem to have waned in recent decades. The reasons for that are doubtless various. No small part has to be the disinterest on the part of faculty in taking on such roles, a disinterest fostered by the premium put on scholarship and participation in the academy. Other factors might be our recent suspicions of elites, the general scramble for place on national boards, and the mandates to structure with sensitivity to the diversity within the church. All militate against the appointment of seminary faculty to board and agency positions. The result was, that on matters of general importance like ecumenism, the agency (GCCUIC in this instance)

lacked substantial contact with United Methodist theological education. Not surprisingly the agency proceeded with its business while the seminaries took their own (ecumenical) tack. The lack of contact by seminary faculty with GCCUIC and GCCUIC's minimal use of seminary faculty may explain, we think, an intellectual divergence on globalization.

GCCUIC had already been working on its connection to theological education prior to the establishment of its seminary committee. With that momentum, the committee, has already gone a long way toward rectifying this gulf between agency and seminary. GCCUIC in turn has greater interest in the preparation of the next generation of ecumenical leadership. Since seminary faculties are quite limited in what they can effectively support, this formula could not and probably should not be adopted by other boards and agencies. And yet, United Methodist boards and agencies may well need to find other non-formal ways of drawing upon the church's intellectual leadership.

At issue here is the church's teaching office. The findings in the survey, the manner of the responses by the schools, efforts by the DOM, and initiatives taken by AUMTS clearly indicate openness and commitment to what is GCCUIC's specific charge, namely ecumenism and interreligious concerns. Given that and GCCUIC's legitimate role in telling its story, how ought the educational missions of seminary and GCCUIC to intersect? The question turns really on the teaching office in Methodism, who exercises it, how it is exercised, how various agencies with legitimate teaching roles interrelate, what incentives and deterrents for cooperative endeavor might exist?

3) GCCUIC's Role in Leadership Formation. In the prior point, we have wondered how GCCUIC (and other agencies) might profit from more ongoing and regular relation with the seminaries and seminary faculty. The inverse also should be mentioned. In particular, should GCCUIC, perhaps in connection with the DOM, concern itself with the way in which ecumenical perspectives and interreligious concerns affect the curriculum and ethos of United Methodist seminaries? Of other seminaries in which United Methodist seminarians are trained? Larger issues are obviously at stake. In what ways do agencies influence seminaries? In what ways should they? How do and how can schools remain current with the church's agendas, policies, and commitments? And since the seminaries intersect with the church through BHEM and DOM, the relation of the various agencies to one another is also in question. How effectively do United Methodist agencies interact where their programmatic mandates overlap?

For GCCUIC, the pertinent question is, "Are seminaries and graduate programs developing a cadre of younger leadership (including seminary faculty) who are committed to and articulate about the ecumenical movement and interreligious dialogue?" Are they educating future clergy to give leadership at the local level (and other levels) in such a way that the life and ministry of all God's people is understood and exercised in an ecumenical and interreligious context? If not, from where will United Methodism draw its ecumenical leadership? We sense that this is a strategic time for GCCUIC (for DOM?) to raise the ecumenical banner in theological education. To do so, of course, raises a further question about the colors to be raised.

4) Globalization, Ecumenism, Interreligious Dialogue. Both the growing commitment of UM schools to globalization and the distance between schools and GCCUIC point to a fourth concern: who sets the ecumenical agenda for the church and in what it consists. The survey indicates what ATS materials also attest, namely that global curricular and extracurricular emphases differ markedly. The global, ecumenical, or interreligious thrust or style of the several UM schools differs. Differences have to do with interests of key faculty members, a school's constituency and make-up, the specific contexts in which it works and local agendas, the international connections the school enjoys. The very terms--global, interreligious, missions, ecumenical--register those divergencies. How do these terms relate? Are they essentially identical? Compatible? What theological meaning do they have? Should they have? If the terms have different meanings and are not essentially identical, how does the church's agenda get set?

What role should GCCUIC play in providing precision in the use of these terms, in identifying United Methodist priorities, in suggesting the appropriate connections between and among them?

Particularly as these terms become central to the curricula--to the way in which schools conceptualize purpose and plan program--their meaning, relation, and relative priority become of concern to the whole connection.

It is our conviction that some such self-conscious discussion of priorities is in order, that these terms do differ, that large issues of direction and policy are at stake. Furthermore, what the seminaries do with these terms matters. Curricular shifts within single schools might not be of general concern; common shifts across the church's seminaries do seem to be a general concern. Globalization apparently constitutes such a common move.

Just to illustrate, we believe that in a diffuse but general orientation to globalization, sustained commitment to and labor on behalf of Christian unity will suffer. It is not our business to argue that Christian unity should be preferred over the other agendas represented in globalization. We do think what is done in the name of globalization--by training the next generation of the church's leaders--will set agenda for the church. Therefore, we think it important to reopen discussion on the nature and thrust of the church's global agenda. What understanding(s) of the nature and purposes of theological education guide(s) these endeavors at globalization? What theologies of church and ministry inform these conceptions? And how do the various indices of unity and diversity--race, communion, sex, liberal/conservative, nationality, region, age, degree program, etc.--intersect? What are the most powerful divisive forces, the most important unitive ones in today's church and world? On which should the seminaries focus? In such a discussion, we presume that various parts of the church, including GCCUIC, would play an important part.

5) Denominational Formation And Ecumenical Formation. The survey indicated that the seminaries, some more than others, have labored to build a global aspect into the structure and rhythms of institutional life. In one instance, it will include the expectation that all students have some global experience, preferably abroad. In other situations, interfaith dialogues give shape to both curriculum and the community's common life. Worship is frequently made a carrier of this commitment; the languages, liturgies, gestures, music, drama, dance, color represented within the community are juxtaposed in creative fashion. Efforts are made to use the implicitly global or ecumenical features of seminary life--the fact that faculty (and students) are drawn from various communions; the presence of international students; consortia, clusters, exchange programs, lectureships, visiting scholars; the ecumenical or academic character of instruction itself. The seminaries are exploring what it means to be global.

At the same time and through the same processes, they take reponsibility for ministerial formation. All train non-Methodists as well as Methodists, so that ministerial formation must be done with sensitivity to the diversity within the school. That acknowledged, these schools do have primary accountability to United Methodism and, of course, primary responsibility for the shaping of its ministry. So, then, it is appropriate to ask how global formation and denominational formation cohere.

That question should eventually come to the fore since throughout the denomination there seem to be increased pressures toward reassertion of United Methodist identity. Motivated by concern over the decline in numbers, the quest for identity turns in a variety of directions but often puts a premium on heightened Wesleyan and Methodist awareness. Can we expect tensions between Wesleyan awareness and global awareness?

An obvious place for global and denominational formation to clash is in worship. In some schools, as we have indicated, worship expresses and dramatizes the community's global awareness. Will that be done, can that be done while acquainting United Methodist students with the new hymnbook and its liturgies? (All the schools were given hymnbooks by the United Methodist Publishing House, in part, for these formative purposes.) The new hymnals and the new global imperative raise afresh a question that each of the schools has had to settle: "How should the common worship life give expression to both the school's primary denominational orientation and the denominational (ethnic, ideological, national, linguistic) pluralism of its student body?" The issue obviously extends beyond worship. What are the ground rules, criteria, or norms by which seminaries allot time, space, importance, etc. to denominational formation and global (or ecumenical) formation?

Concluding Observation

While the GCCUIC committee initially undertook the survey to inform its own work, it recognized the results as of more general interest to those involved in theological formation and to all concerned about the Oneness of the Church. We concur in that conviction but wish to turn some matters back to GCCUIC and the church generally for consideration. In particular, we would invite greater conversation about what 'globalization' means for both seminary and church.

Notes

1. Much of this current interest can be discerned in the official publications of the Association of Theological Schools in the United States and Canada (ATS), particularly its *Bulletin* and *Theological Education*. Notable are "Committee on Global Theological Education," Global Challenges and Perspectives in Theological Education. Programs and Reports, 35th Biennial Meeting. . .June 16-18, 1986 and *Bulletin 37, Part 6* (1986) which includes a significant report by the Committee on Global Theological Education. See also the issues of *Theological Education* entitled "Globalizing Theological Education in North America," XXII (Spring 1986), and "Theological Education in a Religiously Diverse World," XXIII (Supplement, 1987). For indication of the place of globalization in the overall reflection about theological education, see "Reflections on the Literature on Theological Education Published Between 1955-1985," by James M. Gustafson, *Theological Education*, XXIV (Supplement II, 1988), 9-86 and *Christian Identity and Theological Education* by Joseph C. Hough, Jr. and John B. Cobb, Jr. (Chico: Scholars Press, 1985).

2. The term 'we' is used throughout to underscore the role that both Jean Miller Schmidt and I played in the process that is described in the following paragraphs, the shared character of the findings, and joint preliminary analysis

thereof. I take final responsibility for the transposition of those materials into this draft.

3. The survey and the role of Richey and Schmidt therein grew out of a 1986 workshop at the Ecumenical Institute in Bossey, Switzerland devoted to "The Teaching of Ecumenics." The Bossey event had gathered theological faculty from across the world and from the various theological disciplines, among the and under GCCUIC sponsorship, these two American church historians (Schmidt and Richey). They assembled to consider what might be termed the "mainstreaming" of ecumenism, the inclusion of ecumenical perspectives throughout a theological program, teaching "ecumenism" across the curriculum. The findings of this workshop, an effort to reconstruct the several disciplines along ecumenical lines, comprise the October 1987 issue of The Ecumenical Review, "Towards Ecumenical Formation in Theological Schools" and appeared also, in more complete form, as a WCC paperback, *The Teaching of Ecumenics* edited by Samuel Amirtham and Cryis H.S. Moon. A related consultation sponsored by the WCC, held the year previous, had issued in *Ministerial Formation in a Multi-faith Milieu: Implications of Interfaith Dialogue for Theological Education.* These volumes deserve attention in their own right and are not herein summarized.

In making an oral report to GCCUIC on the workshop, Schmidt and Richey, of course, highlighted the importance and excitement of this endeavor to "mainstream" ecumenism, but went on to make a series of observations about the 'ecumenical' state of United Methodist theological education. Relying on the catalogs of the seminaries, they reported on two patterns: (1) the faculty, courses and emphases expressive of long-standing ecumenical/Interreligious commitments; and (2) curricular and extracurricular attention to globalization, apparently inspired by the recent Association of Theological Schools (ATS) and its Task Force on Globalization. Richey and Schmidt asked about the relation between these two patterns and what responsibility GCUIC had to the seminaries (and vice versa) in charting United Methodist policy and program in this general area.

4. Recognizing that this charge affected the domain of DCOM, the Commission had sought and received representation from that division, The Rev. Thomas Starnes.

5. This survey was designed to discover the ecumenical intentions of the schools. Richey and Schmidt and indeed the whole committee are painfully aware that a school's intentions and its actual operations--on global matter as in virtually everything--may differ sharply. Since the purpose of data gathering at this stage was to learn about goals, we were quite content to accept the schools' global self-understandings.

6. The following analysis draws on the suggestions of all members of the committee, the ably constructed notes of the committee's chair and written proposals by Richey, Schmidt, Powers, Reber, and Shinn.

7. The notable exceptions, but clear exceptions, were in the teams constituted for the several General Conference studies and in the preparation of the new hymnal. For both, expertise as well as the support of the entire United Methodist constituency was sought.

8. See Donald W. Shriver, Jr., "The Globalization of Theological Education: Setting the Task," *Theological Education, XXII* (Spring 1986), 15-16.